MW00640615

The Pensive Citadel

The Pensive Citadel

Victor Brombert

FOREWORD BY
CHRISTY WAMPOLE

The University of Chicago Press CHICAGO AND LONDON

The University of Chicago Press, Chicago 60637
The University of Chicago Press, Ltd., London
© 2023 by Victor Brombert
Foreword © 2023 by The University of Chicago
All rights reserved. No part of this book may be used or reproduced in any
manner whatsoever without written permission, except in the case of brief
quotations in critical articles and reviews. For more information, contact
the University of Chicago Press, 1427 East 60th Street, Chicago, IL 60637.
Published 2023
Printed in the United States of America

32 31 30 29 28 27 26 25 24 23   1 2 3 4 5

ISBN-13: 978-0-226-82866-4 (cloth)
ISBN-13: 978-0-226-82867-1 (e-book)
DOI: https://doi.org/10.7208/chicago/9780226828671.001.0001

Library of Congress Cataloging-in-Publication Data

Names: Brombert, Victor, 1923- author. |
Wampole, Christy, 1977- writer of foreword.
Title: The pensive citadel / Victor Brombert ; foreword by Christy Wampole.
Description: Chicago ; London : The University of Chicago Press, 2023. |
Includes index.
Identifiers: LCCN 2023004290 | ISBN 9780226828664 (cloth) |
ISBN 9780226828671 (ebook)
Subjects: LCSH: Brombert, Victor, 1923- | Literature teachers—United States—
Biography. | French teachers—United States—Biography. | Literary historians—
United States—Biography. | College teachers—United States—Biography. |
French literature—History and criticism. | Literature—History and criticism. |
LCGFT: Essays.
Classification: LCC PN75.B69 A3 2023 | DDC 388.408676—dc24
LC record available at https://lccn.loc.gov/2023004290

♾ This paper meets the requirements of ANSI/NISO Z39.48-1992
(Permanence of Paper).

For Bettina, Lauren, and Marc

Contents

Foreword

CHRISTY WAMPOLE

The most interesting scholars are those who, before having entered the university, were already schooled harshly by life. These scholars anchor their reading in the real world, viewing purely theoretical interventions with impatience. A novel or a poem does not exist in a vacuum, free from the vicissitudes of history and the social convulsions these produce. It surfaces from the beautiful havoc of humanity's many moods and weaknesses. The best scholars have lived attentively and endured enough to recognize this. Victor Brombert is such a scholar.

In the following eclectic assemblage of essays, Professor Brombert shows that despite the many hardships he faced during World War II—what he calls Europe's "history-as-nightmare"—and the turbulent postwar period, one can and should treat it all with a certain lightness of touch. In this respect, he is aligned with one of his obvious models, Michel de Montaigne. The sixteenth-century patriarch of the essay wrote of his preferred style in the melding of philosophy and literary expression, "I love the poetic gait, by leaps and gambols. It is an art, as Plato says, light, flighty, daemonic" ("J'aime l'allure poétique, à sauts et à gambades; c'est un art, comme dit Platon, léger, volage, démoniaque"). The heaviness of history is countered in Brombert's writing by the buoyancy of the human spirit. Indeed, he dedicates an entire essay to the question of laughter. But even in broaching heavier subjects, his style resists gravity. He uses the expression "relentless mobility" to describe children he sees running in the Parc Monceau, a phrase that also sums up his own writing and thinking. Of the essay form, Theodor Adorno wrote, "Instead of achieving something scientifically, or creating

something artistically, the effort of the essay reflects a childlike freedom that catches fire, without scruple, on what others have already
done." The following essays do precisely that: they catch fire on the
great books and ideas of the past and flicker with that unbound vigor
the young possess.

It is clear that Brombert heeded the advice of one of his professors
about the writing life: "If ever you write a diary and wish to be read
by posterity, give as many precise details about daily life as possible."
He generously shares such astounding details, like the fact that René
Wellek, founder of Yale's Department of Comparative Literature, had
"prominent buck teeth, which one day were replaced by a sparkling
denture of exemplary regularity." Encountering these rich descriptions
every few pages, we realize that these, perhaps more than monumental
events or headline-making history, are the stuff of life. Many of the following pages offer a celebration of the everyday.

When I arrived at Princeton in 2011, hired in Brombert's old department as a freshly graduated assistant professor, his name was uttered
often and with reverence by my new colleagues. In reading his essays, I
see many similarities between our experiences but also the many ways
the institution and the field of French studies have changed since he was
an assistant professor. What is familiar is the angst of not doing enough
during one's sabbatical, the stage fright before an important lecture, or
the recurrent teaching-related nightmares. But also the good things: the
joy of learning from one's students, of discovering something new each
time you reread a book whose meanings you thought you'd depleted, or
of realizing that you've changed the lives of many through your vocation. Brombert entertains his reader with terrific stories, like the time his
students included his favorite phrases—such as "prolepsis," "diachronic
structures," and "epicurean"—on the bingo cards they made to play
with in class as he lectured. The lesson was punctuated now and then by
shouts of "Brombingo!" Even though they were teasing him, he found
the joke delightful. He exclaims, "My lectures had entered student mythology!" Such stories remind me why I became a teacher and show that
there is something eternal in the student-professor relationship, even as
the university has changed radically over the decades.

Indeed, what has changed since Brombert's early years as an academic outweighs what has remained the same. His reverent descriptions
of his professors at Yale feel to me like vestiges of the past. The legend-

ary status many professors were able to achieve in the twentieth century seems impossible now in our highly fragmented, anti-hierarchical context in which illustriousness is viewed with more than a little cynicism. It is hard to imagine a time when professors could simply teach, without worrying about a self-dilating bureaucracy, the risk of being drawn into the culture wars, or the obligation to publish or perish. It feels nice to immerse oneself in a softer world before students faced so many challenges to their mental health and before the humanities entered a seemingly permanent phase of crisis.

Another important difference is the role of education. In these essays, there is an appreciation of learning for learning's sake, not for achieving some professional goal or increasing one's social status. Students of Brombert's generation read widely, across languages and disciplines, seeking to glean what they could of the world through its literature and philosophy. While this is still true among some students now, most approach their studies with a utilitarian mindset, perhaps because this approach is the most soothing in an increasingly technocratic, anxiety-inducing age.

Brombert describes an academic world before hyperspecialization and particularization, before email and its attendant administrative upsurge, before prudence eclipsed intellectual boldness. In his essays on literature, he reads panoramically and with the eye of a generalist who seems to have read all of what were once called Great Books. He toggles dexterously between Proust and the Bible, between Molière and Leopardi, highlighting shared affinities between compelling minds across the centuries. While everyone else today seems to want to complicate things, Brombert seeks to make them simpler. His project is not to conduct an autopsy on these old tomes, looking for hidden malignancies. The canon, for him, is rather a utopian idea, a project of unification. Because these works speak of life's universal themes—jealousy, love, violence—their lessons are open to everyone, free for the taking. He writes accessibly, not hiding behind jargon or exclusive language. In this respect, his style is invitational, corroborating one's first impression that Brombert is, above all, a generous educator.

In the following pages, one finds intimacy between the professor and his books, direct contact without the intervention of the critics. He simply loves to read. Life and literature always share a border in Brombert's essays. In his school years, truancy allowed him to explore Paris, an activity he describes as a kind of "pre-reading" of Baudelaire's writings on the flâneur. One gets the sense that this figure—the city dweller who absorbs the tumult of the urban space during his aimless wanderings—is also a model for a certain way of reading. He moves through novels and plays in an ambulatory, attentive way, not seeking to discover something specific but to give the text the time and space to leave its impression on him.

The English scholar Arthur Benson once described the essay as "a thing which someone does himself." No better definition applies to these here, each bearing a certain artisanal quality and the signature of its maker. The craftsman's do-it-yourself temperament comes through, especially in "On Rereading" and the bittersweetly titled "The Permanent Sabbatical," a piece that confirms what you suspect as you begin the book; namely, that the craftsman who has been building things all his life is now looking back on what he has made and wondering what will become of his humble offerings. This is a vulnerable state to be in, but Brombert shares his vulnerability with faceless readers, a final gesture of benevolence.

Preface

Variety does not preclude coherence or unity. The essays gathered here, many of which were written in pandemic confinement, touch on a multiplicity of subjects: Shakespeare's Cleopatra, the paradoxical nature of laughter, the art of rereading, the political background to the construction of the Eiffel Tower—and quite a few more. But my title, borrowed from William Wordsworth's ingenious metaphor, "the pensive citadel," clearly refers to the singular world of universities. And indeed, every one of the chapters in this book speaks, obliquely at times, of my half-century-long teaching experience in the humanities.

My nostalgia for those years is explicitly declared by the title of the opening section. These early pages deal largely with my initiation into the world of academia, after escaping from Nazi-occupied Europe and frontline intelligence work—including at Omaha Beach and the Battle of the Bulge. They evoke the lingering sense of alienation that helped me discover my real identity, the determining encounter with an incomparable mentor, the discovery of existentialism, fond memories of early lectures given to very special freshmen, the unpredictable satisfactions of learning from students.

This nostalgic first section evokes, indirectly on occasion, the stages of my academic life: the lasting impact of my exposure to literature and cultural history in the French *lycée*, the initial infatuation with New Criticism when I entered through Yale's portal as a veteran-freshman under the GI Bill, my eventual return to more historically based readings of canonical texts, exposure and resistance to the invasion of "theory," as well as gratifying moments and anxieties as chair of a department in difficult times.

The second section, entitled "The Ludic Mode," stresses the playful aspect of all serious commerce with ideas, of all good teaching and good learning. For learning and teaching prosper where there is intellectual mobility and openness to mutation and change. Montaigne is a model. The chapters in this "ludic" section deal with the endless complexities of laughter, the occasionally cruel inventiveness of the imagination (especially when prey to jealousy), visions and revisions associated with rereading authors, as well as a tribute to transformative books capable of reshaping us.

"The French Connection," the third section, confronts more directly my area of specialization. Molière, Voltaire, Stendhal stand at the center of three distinct, but equally rich periods of French culture—and 1889, the year the Eiffel Tower was built in celebration of the French Revolution, allows for an overview of the political vicissitudes afflicting the nineteenth century, eventually leading to the tragic demise of France's Third Republic in 1940.

Finally, and in temporal opposition to my entrance into an Ivy-league "pensive citadel," the last section, carrying the simple title "The Exit," records my musings on the occasion of my retirement which, in an essay that appeared in the *New Yorker*, I chose to call "The Permanent Sabbatical."

Part I · In Nostalgia

1 · The Pensive Citadel

The early morning hours were the most difficult. Lying in bed in the rented room next to the funeral parlor, I listened to the engines of the limousines lining up in the adjacent driveway, ready to convey their coffined loads to the town's periphery.

Thoughts drifted. It was difficult enough to get started on drizzly days, but even more so when the early rays of the sun intruded with insistent irony. Half awake, I was afraid to fall asleep again and not make it in time all the way to Phelps Hall, where I was to meet my class. I had already been late several times, and as a teaching graduate student I was vulnerable to occasional unannounced inspections. Yet I looked forward to facing my students. I had overheard senior professors talk enviously of sabbaticals. For me, those were at that point only distant mirages. In the present, it was fun to make my freshmen repeat "*C'est rond, c'est long, c'est bon*"—the slightly salacious words uttered with inescapable innuendo by the fictional Mireille in the *Méthode Orale*, our textbook in this intensive language course.

That was more than six decades ago. Presently, the emeritus professor seated on a bench with a missing slat in Parc Monceau, at the edge of the 8th Arrondissement, muses on the actual sabbaticals that punctuated his academic life. A film in rewind. The self takes on the features of a character in a third-person narration. He and I absorb impressions of the park: the fake ruined colonnades, the duck-filled pond, the groomed flowerbeds, the couples snuggling on nearby benches, the employees munching their luncheon sandwiches on the grass, the neoclassical rotunda that was once a toll station at the entrance of Paris and now houses public toilets.

On my bench, I ponder the meaning of the word "sabbatical." It pleases me to think that beyond the obvious reference to an extended academic leave every seven years for the purpose of renewal and research, the word had more venerable meanings associated with the number seven: the seventh day of creation, when the Lord rested; the seventh day of the week, meant to be a day of repose, reverence, and spiritual meditation; the seventh year during which the land was to remain untilled and allowed to rest according to religious law, and all debts remitted. As for the witches' sabbath, it carried distinct perverse and therefore seductive undertones, referring as it does to demonic nocturnal revels. Somehow sabbatical had become for me a metaphor evoking the broader enticements of life.

In a sense, my academic existence began in a sabbatical mode: an entire year on a Fulbright fellowship in Rome to finish my dissertation on Stendhal, the great lover of Italy. In the immediate post-World War II years, Rome was still awaking from nightmarish times, recorded in neorealistic films such as Roberto Rossellini's *Rome, Open City* and Vittorio De Sica's *The Bicycle Thief*. Peace had returned, but Italians were profoundly divided as the new Cold War intensified. Riot squads in jeeps—the *celere* created by the minister of the interior, Mario Scelba, known as the "Iron Sicilian"—were protecting the US Embassy and suppressing turbulent left-wing street protests as well as neofascist rallies. But by 1950, Rome once again began to transcend contemporary history, and the newly wed Fulbright couple, in quest of historic perspectives and poetic sensations, was discovering the legendary hills of the Eternal City, but also the more popular quarters, as Bettina and I followed the footsteps of Stendhal, using his writings about Rome as guide and inspiration.

Our walks often led us up to the church of San Pietro in Montorio on the Janiculum. There was decidedly no escape from Stendhal. As I directed my view toward the multilayered monuments of Rome, and beyond them, to the Pincio and the gardens of villa Borghese, I recalled vividly the opening pages of Stendhal's autobiographical *Life of Henry Brulard*, which I had recently examined with pencil in hand. In this magical overture, the author finds himself on a sunny and slightly windy fall day near the same San Pietro in Montorio, perhaps on the same spot where we stood. At a great distance, he distinguishes Monte Albano and Castel Gandolfo, but his eyes focus on the topography and the monuments of the great city, the church of Santa Maria Maggiore, the Tiber, Monte Cavallo, the orchard of a monastery, the Appian Way—a vast panorama with its architectural layers of time blending in his imagination with the vistas of his own life, which he sets out to survey with bemusement and quasi-paternal affection while fully aware of aging and mortality. The historical times of ancient and modern Rome blend with the temporal layers of his personal history in these lyric reminiscences that come to the surface in their transient simultaneity. Memory and reveries exchange their riches, while he begins to see himself as a fictional character.

· · ·

In later years, I was often teased by my Italian friends about the string of sabbaticals that made it possible for us to return to Italy and renew our friendships. What they did not suspect was that pangs of guilt were never absent from these festive months. Did I use my time well? Did the research and writing make any progress? Dangers are lurking during any moveable feast. How is one to maintain even the semblance of self-discipline once away from daily tasks? The very illusion of a vacation comes with a nagging sense of vacuity. I was not the first to experience the occasional disarray of sabbaticals, the self-blame that goes with feeling ineffective, or even halted in one's project about which growing doubts arise. Too many books available in the reading room of the library. One can so easily be distracted. And often the book one really needs is elsewhere. Another occasion to be sidetracked. Leaving the Biblioteca Nazionale in Florence to consult the catalogue of the Institut Français further down the river Arno, I improvised more than one lengthy detour uphill by way of San Miniato, near the Piazzale Michelangelo from where one enjoys a commanding view that rivals the one from Rome's Janiculum.

Daydreaming on my bench in Parc Monceau, now that I find myself on permanent sabbatical, I see quite clearly that for me there was never anything frivolous about the notion of "sabbatical." It had become the unexpected metaphor for the range of satisfactions and stresses of the life I had chosen, but principally for the joy of teaching and the welcome anguish of writing.

I have long been fond of Wordworth's poem—a sonnet in defense of the sonnet's constricting form—in which the poet writes in praise of desired constraints and even imprisonment. I remember the first three lines of the poem:

> Nuns fret not at their convent's narrow room;
> And hermits are contented with their cells;
> And students with their pensive citadels . . .

"Pensive citadels" leaves me dreamy. It provides the title of this book. I could not myself have come up with that striking formula.

Yet something like it, or a feeling akin to it, came to mind the day in 1946 when I first glimpsed the towers of Yale, with still keen memories of the Normandy landings and the endless snowfalls during the Battle of the Bulge. Here indeed, next to New Haven's spacious Green with its three denominational churches, was a citadel, a stronghold, a fortress. But not for war.

About my life in two such citadels I have long wished to write a book as sunny as certain wines are sunny. Harkness Tower in New Haven and later the bell tower of Nassau Hall in Princeton had become for me emblems of contentment after the war years and the experience of battlefields. I wanted to write about a privileged profession—privileged especially in those postwar years, but now so fraught with frustrations. I wished to explain why I would gladly live those five decades of teaching all over again. Yet I knew that I would never write an effusive book of that kind—except by indirection, in oblique and even playfully ironic ways that would shun sentimentality and self-congratulatory preachiness. "Playful" was perhaps the key word. It made me think of the importance of playfulness in teaching. It brought home that seeing the other side of any question is at the heart of good thinking. This is perhaps the reason I am so drawn to Montaigne, determined to give audience to the opposite of his own just-stated opinion, and whose *Essays* are such an outstanding demonstration of mental agility.

"The Joy of Teaching"—that was decidedly not a title I would adopt. Such a title was bound to invite ironic smiles and dismissive comments. Yet that joy is what has remained with me as I recall those years—that incomparable exaltation when intellectual closeness can almost be physically felt, when the classroom hour seems to be lived like a performance in a time unlike any other, and one is happy to learn while teaching. I was often reminded of Chaucer's Oxford clerk:

"And gladly wolde he lerne, and gladly teche."

I was struck by this line in *The Canterbury Tales* when I myself was a freshman.

It is not easy to talk, or for that matter to write, about what matters most. The French have a word for the bashfulness or reticence one feels about intense emotions. That word is *pudeur*, connoting various forms of modesty, discretion, reserve, decorum, about intimate subjects. My favorite metaphor for the years spent in academia—the sabbatical years— stems from just such *pudeur*, the notion of "sabbatical" serving to some extent as protective screen. For the sabbatical years comprise in my memory all the activities and byproducts of my teaching years, including the periods of real leaves when I haunted the libraries of Rome, Paris, and Florence, debated theories and ideologies in then still Communist Hungary, explored Vienna under the shadow of the Iron Curtain, attended symposia in Nice or Perugia, or basked in the Madeira sun while at work on a book.

Who would deny that a dash of self-indulgence goes into the classroom performance: taking in the students' timely laughter, relishing appreciative smiles, even cultivating a preliminary stage fright that intensifies the theatrical silence preceding the first words of the lecture? But those were trivial matters that mattered to me only. They were the private satisfactions of a private stage, and they had little to do with what I felt to be the serious business of the liberal arts (an expression never heard in my French schooldays), nor with reverence for the humanities, which meant not only loving one's subject but valuing the precious contact with others—precious because it facilitated tolerance for new ideas as well as that friction which produces the spark.

Yet teaching came with anxieties, magnified in some recurrent nightmares. In one of these, I arrive disheveled, at dawn, in a sputtering, decrepit taxicab just as my stampeding group of undergraduates rush out of the main door of the hall. A released torrent. I try to stem the flow. I threaten, I try to cajole. They are already beyond the reach of my voice. They have not even recognized me. I stand in the street with my palms outstretched, powerless, rejected. I am a total failure.

In the other bad dream, I am lecturing in a large, increasingly dark, pseudo-Gothic hall. Most of the students hide their faces behind a college newspaper. Some of them yawn loudly. Others snicker without apparent reason and then sing scabrous songs. I myself gradually shrink in size, while trying in vain to look impressive. Once again, I feel inept and rejected.

Insecurities about my teaching gnawed at me sporadically all those years, not only in my sleep. They also led me to ask myself what makes a good teacher. Clearly it was not just the ability to prevent students from running away. Nor were erudition, brilliance, and wit exclusive or even necessary prerequisites. They could in fact prove to be oppressive and repelling, especially—as is often the case—when accompanied by arrogance and disdain. Models of truly good teachers came to mind, mentors I had admired and who had inspired me. But none was more outstanding than Henri Peyre, the legendary professor of French literature at Yale (but also a charismatic figure nationally in the humanities) whose intense presence radiated love of his subject and confidence. The confidence he radiated was not in himself; it was in the as yet unproven abilities of his students. Undergraduates and doctoral candidates alike listened to him with ravishment. They loved his scintillating presentations, his verbal resources, his unpredictable digressions ranging from Greek mythology to Dostoevskyan soul-searching, French viticulture, the political theories of Guicciardini, Baudelaire's poems on lesbianism, the aberrations of the Inquisition . . . It was a heady feast. We relished his warm voice with its ever so faint meridional inflections. Much of the time, one felt, he surprised even himself. He knew more about Hellenism in European culture or English Romantic poetry than many a specialist in those fields. We punningly referred to him as "notre Peyre à tous"—our common father. Even his teasing was benign. And he loved to tease, but without a trace of condescension. We sensed that he took interest in each and every one of us, while respecting our freedom.

As I now look back to what has come to be known at Yale as the "Peyre years"—he chaired the French department for twenty-five years—I see that in his example there was also a crucial lesson for the future teacher and next chairman. For Peyre did not believe that the function of a teacher in the humanities was to transmit facts or factual knowledge as the "truth," expecting them to be regurgitated at some future exam, but to inspire, excite, open horizons, and provide intellectual pleasure of the highest order. The point was not to expect students to repeat and imitate but to help them discover their own possibilities. That was a precious lesson. But years passed before I developed my own voice, since I had from the beginning taken Peyre as my model.

• • •

My occasional nightmares about teaching seemed to me real enough; they projected lingering doubts about my abilities. But I understood even then that, in an amplified and grotesque manner, they offered proof of my enthusiasm. And more disturbing than such ephemeral dreams were the mounting threats to the whole enterprise of the humanities—beginning in the 1960s, and intensifying during the years of the Vietnam War. It started with the invasion of "theory" and critical methodologies, largely imported from Paris, that inflicted on us in rapid succession doctrinaire trends and fashions carrying such names as postmodernism, structuralism, poststructuralism, and finally deconstruction, the most devastating in its effects. French departments were largely instrumental in making known the distinguished names of Ferdinand de Saussure, Claude Lévi-Strauss, Roman Jakobson, Jacques Lacan, Roland Barthes, Gérard Genette, Jacques Derrida, Paul de Man. Students and epigones eager to ride on these innovative tides—most often without true familiarity with the works involved—would no longer write a paper without peppering their footnotes with references to their revered intercessors to the Truth, and in the process displayed not bold new thinking, but epidemic conformity. French studies soon contaminated other fields in the humanities. And with a vengeance. For these innovative and often conflictual fashions had one feature in common: they challenged the validity of the very notion of the "humanities," discrediting their moral foundation and moral claims and announcing the necessary demise of the humanistic ethos, irredeemably corrupted—so we were told—by its bourgeois, elitist, and hegemonic nature.

The assault on the humanities from within the humanities was carried out by means of an arsenal of rhetorical devices, technical words, and pretentious circumlocutions. A real jargon. One heard a lot about "aporia," "tropes," "metonymy." "Narratological" and "narratology" were highly honored, and so was the "diegetical" element of "textuality." In this "diacritical" perspective, historical, social, and biographical considerations were out, definitely out. But "intertextuality" was valued as a way of "evacuating" the author, and the term "undecidable" was mouthed in an almost mythical fashion. Those with some French at their command delighted in the word *béance*, a vacuity at the core of every textual product, a wide-open space, a gaping hole that invited the critic to speculate on what was of necessity unspoken or unspeakable. It was a rhetorical carnival in which everything, especially the most obvious, had to be unmasked or decoded, transforming learned meetings into hermetic gatherings where the new mandarins talked exclusively to themselves.

A seminar I periodically attended, led by one of the gurus of deconstruction, debated at length whether a given figure of speech in a work by Denis Diderot, a luminary of the French Enlightenment, was a metaphoric metonymy or a metonymic metaphor. In the process, Diderot's distinctive voice got lost. The author was no longer heard, he no longer counted.

The death of the author, the death of the novel, the death of literature. We heard a lot about death in those days. Ultimately, the sterile and predictable stress on textual "self-referentiality" began to erode the joy of literary studies. Worse still, a mood of suspicion and distrust increasingly affected younger colleagues and graduate students as a direct consequence of ideological hostility from devotees of one dogmatic theory against the converts to another, and their combined contempt for those who, in their eclectic tolerance, dared have no "theory" at all. ("Eclectic" had become a distinctly pejorative term.)

Humorlessness and glum resentments were much in evidence the weekend a Parisian guru appeared at a conference with a contingent of young French followers. The Parisian circus, they were dubbed. But they were not entertaining. When the guru was challenged (I may have been the culprit) about his patent lack of interest in the pleasure literature can give, he angrily exploded: "What do I care about pleasure? I don't want to be happy, I want to be right!" ("Peu me chaut d' être heureux, je veux avoir raison!") The trouble was that everyone wanted to be right. *Avoir raison.* Even our students grew intractable as they tried to impose their critical ideologies on one another. Addiction to doctrines had become contagious.

Those were of course the years of political discontent, the years of the Vietnam War and its aftermath, when university governance was contested and the wind of rebellion blew across many a campus. Even some colleagues could be heard making feverish speeches in support of student demands, trying their best to sound youthful by adopting the rhetoric of revolution. The burning question was student participation in the business of governing the university. For the more radically minded, all governance was henceforth to come "from below." Even the business of teaching was affected. A young medievalist recently recruited from the then-revolutionary ambiance of Columbia University proudly reported to his new chairman that at his initial meeting with his class he asked his students to vote on what they wished to study, and to decide—they who had not yet read a single medieval text—what the syllabus should be. Not only the joy of studies had departed.

Now, more than half a century later, the inebriations and excesses of those years appear softened by the humor of remembrance. And surely there are more serious threats to the humanities at present, more serious even than the undermining of core courses, the discrediting of traditional canons, and the proliferation of self-enclosed new subdisciplines. This is a period of much distress for university teachers in the humanities, who witness the dismantling of programs, the replacements of tenure and tenure-track positions by overworked adjuncts and part-timers, as well as diminishing enrollments in humanities majors. In addition, a technological and media-oriented culture has affected the universities, seduced by the promises—economic and didactic—held out by online education, potentially so damaging to the dialogic and collaborative nature of good teaching and learning. For discussion is of the essence, and good teaching—developing intellectual mobility and availability to new ideas—requires partners and contact. Eye contact. Physically felt responses. Expressions of doubt, skepticism, irony on faces that one can see. The indispensable contact that modifies what one is saying, that corrects one's approach. Ultimately a joint effort.

•   •   •

The sabbatical years—the metaphor is extendable. Retirement too can be considered a sabbatical. But the emeritus must be careful to shun all pathos, all self-pity. Under no condition is he to make a habit of appearing like a revenant to the departmental corridors in search of welcoming faces—a sure recipe for unhappiness. Even the few lingering graduate students, slow to finish their dissertations, will eventually disappear. As for the young new colleagues, they do not begin to suspect that the unknown person looking so lost walking past the lounge was not very long ago a silhouette familiar to many. Avoiding the distress of retirement is not so difficult in this profession, after all. One need not resort to eccentric hobbies. One need not even change one's habits so very much. Carrels in libraries remain available, and so are work projects that involve, as Flaubert might say, the mania for "aligning words." And if the book does not get written, there is not even the excuse that the classroom, office hours, and committees devour one's precious time. So, back to the desk and to the pen! Flaubert comes to mind once more. In one of his letters, he claims that "sentences" were the true adventures of his life—the sentences he committed to paper, as well as the sentences in the many books he read. He described himself as an *homme plume*, a "penman," a human pen. That image, when I think of it, reminds me that, long before I dreamt that I might one day commit anything to paper myself, fountain pens had been a passion of mine, ever since in my childhood I touched them on my father's desk, where I admired their various shapes and designs next to the rocker blotter, the morocco leather container with the dark marble balls, and the many-sized pads of paper.

The sabbatical metaphor could be stretched farther still. All of life might be considered a sabbatical. And why not? The Spanish playwright Pedro Calderón de la Barca wrote of life as a dream—a concept not unknown to antiquity. Some of us may prefer to view life as a privileged span of time granted us, with the attending sadness of knowing that, like all sabbaticals, it must come to an end. For no matter what hardships we encounter, to be alive is to be a survivor. Home from the war, I have often thought of Odysseus's return to Ithaca. Suspicious of the cult of heroes, repelled by the gory scenes of the *Iliad*, I far preferred the story told in the *Odyssey*, the homecoming of resourceful Odysseus to his island, the return from the world of slaughter and monsters back to the world of human beings, back to the marriage bed and to his Penelope. Odysseus the survivor.

The return to Ithaca. I have also come to understand it as a return to health. In my imagination it became associated with the joy of convalescence. If only, I thought, one could always live with a sense of revival, such as, when health is restored, the simplest pleasures count again: a glass of cool water, a succulent fruit, a movement of air caressing the bare forearm. How to keep the renewal of convalescence alive? I knew early on that such satisfactions depended on the awareness of one's fragility, on the perception of finding oneself at all times between vulnerable states of being. Convalescence could also be a metaphor. It was after almost bleeding to death when violently thrown off his horse, that the slowly convalescing Montaigne felt for the first time liberated from the fear of dying, and discovered—as he put it—that his trade and art was living.

•   •   •

Montaigne in Parc Monceau, Stendhal on the Janiculum. Books and their authors were the inevitable counterpoint to my musings on the sabbatical years that began with my Fulbright fellowship in Rome, and even earlier when, fresh from the battle zones of France and Germany, I entered through the gates of a pensive citadel, together with many other World War II veterans. Books and their authors charted the years that followed with their shifting moods. It seems only logical, if I am to write about those years, that it would be not along strictly factual and chronological lines but in an overlapping and to some extent oblique fashion, around the books I myself wrote, as well as those that determined my desire to write them.

I have long been aware of the shuttle going back and forth between lived experience and works of the imagination. They color each other. No clear line of demarcation exists between them. Lived life and art exchange their resources. So also, is there a constant shuttle between the present and the past. Long ago I realized that what I had witnessed, felt, or imagined was diversely represented in the novels and poems I came to know, and that it was precisely this crafted representation that allowed me to better grasp my own experiences. Already as a disobedient and secretive boy, when I was hiding at forbidden hours to plunge again into the book that enraptured me at the time, I was somehow aware that I was also making discoveries about myself.

2 · Between Two Worlds

THE PORTAL

So this is it, I kept repeating to myself as we drove past the Green with its three churches. The driver pointed to a tower, saying, "There's the Old Campus." The word "campus" reminded me of the elderly fellow refugee on the Spanish banana freighter who urged me, if ever we reached the promised land of the United States, to attend college there. An American college. With a campus. These words he spoke with reverence.

So this is it, I kept thinking. I was already familiar with the Green, as I was with another tower, the one of the administration building where my interview had taken place several weeks earlier, shortly after my discharge from the army. A taxi had then also conveyed me from the New Haven railroad station, which remained memorable, not because of its architecture (although I eventually learned that it was listed as a Historical Place), but because that is where a sudden impulse had made me get off at the last moment from a halted train, as I was returning to New York after an interview at Harvard. I did what I only saw happen in movies. I suddenly remembered that there was another well-known university here. I jumped off the train as it was about to leave the station, found a taxi, and asked to be taken to the Yale administration hall where admissions interviews take place. It was late in the afternoon. An arrow on a large poster marked "Veterans" helped me locate the correct floor. My interviewer had also been in the Battle of the Bulge. Shrapnel in his head. We had a long talk. A week later I received the good news. And here I was entering Yale as a twenty-three-year-old freshman, together with a contingent of veterans who were admitted to a term beginning exceptionally in the month of March. Among them, I later found out, was one George H. W. Bush, whom I never got to know, although I might have sat next to him in a lecture course. We were an unusually large class.

I told my driver that I was coming to Yale under the GI Bill, that I had lost five years because of the war, and that I was looking for an inexpensive but clean hotel. He knew, so he said, just the place for me—a decent, unassuming place—and he drove me to what I learned is Chapel Street. The hotel was the Duncan. Unassuming indeed: an indifferent lobby, an old elevator, a viewless room. And a rather unfriendly welcome. But I was not to be disheartened, feeling fortified by the terms of the GI Bill grant: my tuition fully paid, a book allowance and an additional $75 monthly in cash—not a mean amount at the time.

The rest was provided by my father, and that rest allowed me to stay several nights in a hotel and plan on renting a room in town. For life with roommates did not thrill me after the long stretch of army life. I longed for privacy in the shower and on the toilet. I was encouraged in my plan, having learned that the university, overcrowded by the arrival of so many additional students, was actually pleased to see some of them seek lodging in town. The idea of living off campus pleased me for other reasons. It would give me the illusion of independence, and as my mother might somewhat preciously have said, if I had the *bonne fortune* of meeting someone attractive . . .

I knew nothing of New Haven as yet besides the railroad station, the Green, one side of the Old Campus, one administration building, and now the Duncan Hotel. I had not even glimpsed the two reddish sandstone hills where I would in years to come take many a walk. My only walk on this first day, after I settled in my cheerless room, was of an exploratory nature in search of permanent quarters. I did not have to walk far. Next to a funeral parlor, on that same Chapel Street, I stopped in front of a two-family house with a wooden porch and a sign advertising a room for rent. The shabbily dressed woman with an angular face who opened the door seemed to be a creation of Norman Rockwell. I decided then and there that she was a perfect exemplar of a Puritan whose ancestors might have come on the Mayflower—only to discover sometime later that she was of Polish extraction. So much for my astute deciphering of the American melting pot at that time.

The pseudo-Puritan landlady and I discussed the rental, and we agreed that I would move into the room two days later. I was now ready to begin life as a freshman at Yale. Although I remember with clarity my arrival at the station, the exchange with the taxi driver, the fleeting view of the Green, the dim hotel room, and the negotiation with the landlady, what remains a blank is my induction into the university and whatever ceremony took place to welcome our group of war veterans. The mere fact, however, that more than half a century later I resort to the word "induction" in referring to this memory gap suggests to me that army expressions were still associated with this initiation into the radically different new experience as an overage undergraduate that was to take place between Phelps Tower, the classrooms of William Harkness Hall, and the fortress of the Sterling Library. The recent past was still very much with me; I could not readily dismiss lingering images of landing in a jeep on Omaha Beach, watching the carpet bombing of Saint-Lô from a reconnaissance half-track, interrogating prisoners, and later facing German Tiger tanks in the freezing Ardennes during the Battle of the Bulge.

A STATELESS HERITAGE

The room on Chapel Street displayed a Spartan simplicity: an adequate bed, a smallish desk, a little table for my portable phonograph. No private bathroom, of course; but the one to be shared with next-door tenants was kept reasonably clean. On my phonograph I repeatedly played Beethoven's Eroica symphony and arias sung by Ezio Pinza. I did not tire of listening to excerpts from Bellini's *Norma* and Mozart's *Don Giovanni*. Occasional giggles coming from the adjacent room put my imagination to work.

Soon I developed the habit of going to a neighborhood bar between ten and eleven at night, ordering poached eggs on toast, and watching boxing on TV. The rounds were punctuated by commercials for Gillette razorblades. Feel sharp, be sharp. I kept promising myself that I would leave after the next round. The action was often sluggish. From round to round I just sat there. The poached eggs were gone long ago; so was the brownie. The Shelley poem and the Platonic dialogue still waited for me, unread, on my desk. Occasional visitors warmed and cheered up my room, making me forget that when I raised the blind, I stared at the wall of the funeral parlor almost within arm's reach. Yet when I was alone, I faced my solitude and the uneasy sensation of remaining an alien. I did not quite know where I belonged.

It was not a new feeling. My parents, stateless exiles after the Bolsheviks came to power, held largely meaningless Nansen passports issued by the League of Nations as identity documents after Lenin revoked the citizenships of all Russian expatriates. As a result of my family's double exile—first to Germany, then to France—I grew up with three languages. English came later. Eventually, my parents experienced a third exile, the last leg of their journey, when we managed to escape from Nazi-occupied France, via Spain, to the United States. It was during this adventurous escape on a banana freighter carrying well over one thousand refugees across a U-boat–infested Atlantic (the ship was torpedoed and sank on the way back to Spain) that I first keenly felt myself living between two worlds. The seventeen-year-old I was at the time of those six weeks of errant crossing stared endlessly at the dark waters rushing by and at the sea foam, his thoughts fixed on what was left behind and on what lay ahead. Homer's wine-dark sea and Poseidon's anger came to mind—memories of lycée lessons. But the real preoccupation was not literary; it was the question: where did I really belong? I was at the same time yearning to reach some destination, yet already nostalgic for what I had left.

The chaos of languages all around me did not help. We were camping on deck of the cargo boat in our oldest clothes, sleeping in lifeboats or on unhygienic cots in the smelly hold. It would have been hard for the Spanish sailors to imagine that many of the people they were transporting to distant shores were respected professionals, artists, scholars, well-established business people. Most of them were Jewish, and they came from a variety of European nations; but the crew probably did not quite know what a Jew was.

My own personal attachment to France remained surprisingly undiminished, despite the shameful behavior of so many during the Occupation, the anti-Semitic measures of Vichy, the complicities in sending countless individuals into deportation and almost assured death—and later the epidemic of denunciations I had witnessed at the time of the Liberation, when I landed as a Ritchie Boy in Normandy with the US Army. All my schooling, my friends and adolescent adventures, all my sentimental involvements and youthful dreams, were associated with life in France. And so I seemed destined, for years to come, to defend France when in the presence of skeptical Americans, and to extol the United States in discussions with unfriendly Europeans—in either case occasionally against my own better judgment. I even began to see the positive side of finding myself so often between two worlds. Feeling unsettled seemed to help me discover an identity of my own.

Now that I entered Yale, the question was: would I feel like an alien in this university, which under normal circumstances I would never have attended?

VOICES FROM THE PODIUM

More alive than images of neo-Gothic towers and colonial-style residential colleges, more sharply outlined even than newly befriended fellow students, were faculty figures encountered in the early days and embedded in the memory of the scholar I hoped to become. Some served as models. Others taught me what not to emulate. Some made a fleeting impression. A dramatically inclined Professor Richard Purdy gave me my first notion of how Chaucer's Middle English might have been pronounced, thrilling me as he recited some onomatopoeic, or sound-suggestive, verses from the Nun's Priest's merry tale about the rooster Chantecleer—describing a crowd rushing after the predatory fox to the blowing of trumpets and the collective shrieking and whooping of the pursuers.

Other teachers are remembered for less poetic reasons. A course on Shakespeare, offered by one of the college masters, enlisted assistants to read and grade papers, which were returned, no matter on what subject, with a grade (in blue pencil), but not a single comment. What a contrast to the young French instructor, Jean Bruneau (later to become an acclaimed authority on Flaubert), who wrote incisive observations in the margin of every paragraph, and then an abundant commentary at the conclusion of the paper. A lesson I did not forget.

And there was the mustached, benign-looking philosophy professor Brand Blanshard, great proponent of the rational life, who from the distant podium could be seen rhythmically raising, first his right hand, then his left, as though weighing ponderous matters, while inevitably uttering, in mild tones, the ritualistic formula, "on the one hand . . . on the other . . ." His serene, expressionless face seemed to offer evidence of objectivity and equanimity.

The most crowded lecture course, as I recall, was Ralph Gabriel's on "American Democratic Thought" (I often wondered in later years whether our classmate George H. W. Bush attended and listened).

Personally, I preferred the modern English literature course given by Eugene Waith, a younger, urbane person, familiar with the European scene. Sophisticated and interested in modernity, he seemed to know every aspect of Kurt Weill's and Bertolt Brecht's *Three Penny Opera*. For him I wrote papers on the jungle episode in Evelyn Waugh's *A Handful of Dust* and on a minor figure in E. M. Forster's *Passage to India* that I have kept in a three-ring notebook. This course also revealed to me Virginia Woolf's great experimental novel *To the Lighthouse*, which, many years later, I taught with such pleasure and even wrote about. Waith was sensitive, open-minded, wholly nonideological, and eventually befriended me when I became a colleague holding forth on the French novel in the same lecture hall.

And there was also the more conventional, mildly pontificating Frederick Pottle, great authority on the Boswell papers, whose ex cathedra pronouncements on English Romantic poetry were slightly soporific in their morning effect, but who made me discover the dramatic monologues of Robert Browning, and in particular his poem carrying the lengthy title "The Bishop Orders His Tomb at Saint Praxed's Church"—a poem I reread recently, and which impressed me again by how much it says about the spirit of the Italian Renaissance, as the imaginary bishop rambles on, addressing his nephews (in reality his sons!), ordering basalt for the slab of his tomb and an epitaph in choice classical Latin.

It was a little later, during my second year at Yale, that I encountered the gurus of literary criticism. Cleanth Brooks was the high priest of what had come to be known as the New Criticism. No matter what poem he was analyzing, the words "texture" and "structure" were sure to be pronounced with reverence. But the truly incantatory terms of his lexicon, his inescapable mantra, were the almost mystically enunciated terms "irony" and "paradox." He regularly excoriated critics guilty of what he called the paraphrastic heresy—meaning thereby the sin of accounting for a text by describing its meaning. The gods of his poetic pantheon were the English metaphysical poets John Donne and Andrew Marvell. Idiosyncratically, I was indisposed from the start by Cleanth Brooks's Southern accent, which reminded me—even though his tone was consistently mild and courteous—of the army sergeant in basic training whose commands I had so much trouble understanding. But what really troubled me was the New Critic's indifference, if not downright hostility, to the historical, cultural, and political context of literary works.

And there was also the formidable Bill Wimsatt. How could one forget him? His gigantic frame and sharp, polemical mind struck awe into his listeners. He snorted loudly to punctuate his objections, often referring to Aristotle and Longinus. The preferred butt of his sarcasms was what he called the "intentional fallacy"—namely, any attempt to explicate a text in terms other than formalistic or objective. His ire was sure to be aroused by any reference to biographical details, which he considered frivolous external information. Yet despite his huge dimensions and dismissive snorting, Bill Wimsatt was gregarious and gentle at heart, regularly meeting students—and for that matter anyone interested in debating ideas—at George and Harry's, a favorite student haunt on Wall Street. By a twist of circumstance, Wimsatt became the adviser for my senior honors thesis on T. S. Eliot—not the most comfortable challenge in my undergraduate career.

Less colorful and less polemical, the Czech scholar René Wellek seemed to me, by background and by training, to possess a far broader erudition than either Brooks or Wimsatt. A disciple of the Prague school of linguistics, he was already an international voice in literary criticism when he arrived on the Yale scene at about the same time I resumed my studies after the war. It is he who created the Department of Comparative Literature— although not immediately. His first home was the Department of Slavic Languages and Literatures, under whose auspices he gave a course on Russian literature that I attended. I was struck by his prominent buck teeth, which one day were replaced by a sparkling denture of exemplary regularity. In his enthusiasm for his subject, he was given to vehement gestures and clumsy movements which on one occasion made him stumble off the podium as he was striding forth and back while lecturing on Gogol's *Dead Souls*. He was in the habit of rapidly repeating the last three words of sentences he considered important. His historical and literary memory was astounding. Behind his self-effacing manner, Wellek was however a man of strong convictions. As a comparatist, he was opposed, many years later, to the appointment of Paul de Man, whom he considered an enemy of the historical method.

Certain words or opinions heard in a classroom still resound. Whatever made me take a course in English social history given by a professor whose name I choose to remember as that of Trevelyan? He was of course not the great British historian George Macauley Trevelyan, but the course was inspired by the latter's survey of social life in England from Chaucer to Queen Victoria. The topics included the rise of the rural middle class, the decline of the craft guilds, the growth of London, slums and the death rate, the importance of Deism, the legalization of trade unions. Much time was spent on the diaries of John Evelyn and Samuel Pepys. Of all this wealth of material I remember the barest outlines—not a single concrete fact. Only one of our professor's sentences, only one piece of advice, remained with me: "If ever you write a diary and wish to be read by posterity, give as many precise details about daily life as possible." I often pondered this advice years later, as I was writing a wartime memoir and puzzled about some precise fact. For instance, did my army dog tag carry the letter "J" or the letter "H" to indicate that I was Jewish? In either case, not exactly the kind of information to carry around my neck if I were captured by the Germans. But in the event of death on the battlefield—so I was told when I objected—the Quartermaster Corps needed to know what chaplain to call.

DELICATE QUESTIONS

One day my father asked me casually whether there were any Jews on the faculty. The question vaguely annoyed me. To the best of my knowledge, the philosopher Paul Weiss was the only Jewish full professor at Yale, and probably the first one—at least in the humanities. But why did my father's question annoy me? Was it because I did not wish to admit to myself that nasty prejudices survived in the supposedly enlightened world of the university I attended? And prejudices did survive, even though they most often made their appearance in an oblique fashion. As late as the 1960s, I heard an English professor declare, in talking about a Jewish refugee who happened to be an excellent Wordsworth scholar, that with an accent such as his, one could not possibly teach "Intimations of Immortality" or *The Prelude*. It was a painful reminder of an assertion famously made by Charles Maurras, the intellectual head of the extreme right Action Française movement, that a Jew could not conceivably understand Racine.

I explained to my father that, at any rate, the student body was changing rapidly, that there were quite a few Jewish students, especially among the veterans of the recent war, who, like me, benefited from the

GI Bill of Rights—a fact attested to by the numerous Ashkenazi names on our class list published a few years ago under the title "We of '48." But no one seemed to make an issue of this change at the time. And when in my English class we read Chaucer's "Prioress's Tale" describing in detail the wanton murder of a Christian child by a "cursed Jew" who cut its throat and threw it in a pit filled with excrement, not one student raised any question (I myself remained silent), even though the bigoted story reflects an age-old libel—namely, the belief that Jews kidnapped and ritualistically killed Christian children to use their blood for the baking of Passover matzos. No one spoke up.

Once again between two worlds. Upon safely reaching the promised land of liberty, I had been surprised by attitudes toward Black people, who were then still called "colored," or by other more derogatory terms. Their color was evident, but they were visible mainly as domestic help, as waiters, elevator men, porters, or shoeshine boys. I was further astonished by the total segregation in the wartime army. I do not believe that in my three years in training camps and in battle zones I ever came close to Black soldiers except for occasional dealings with service and supply units.

Something troubled me more, however. I knew about the discriminating quota system in the immigration laws favoring people of Nordic or Anglo-Saxon heritage, laws that made it difficult for people from certain countries to obtain immigration visas to the United States. But now I also heard of university policies affecting certain religious and ethnic groups, notably Jews. Even though there was no denying that France had its own brand of anti-Semitism, French universities and elite professional schools, before the Nazi invasion, admitted candidates on the basis of merit and competitive exams. No questions asked about religion or ethnic background. But when I landed in the States a few months before Pearl Harbor and looked for a junior college to improve my English, I recall being repeatedly irked by the inevitable question on every application about my religious affiliation. I was inclined to answer: none. And that would have been the truth. But I was advised that such an answer implied that I might be an atheist. And that in turn would make me suspect of having extreme left-wing sympathies, of being a radical or, even worse, a Communist. Not recommended for one who was applying for citizenship.

I felt vaguely betrayed. Here I thought that we had escaped from a world of Nazi-inspired checking and controls. My parents and I were especially sensitive on the subject. The Vichy regime, under which we had lived and survived for over a year before escaping via Spain, had instituted a dreaded office of Jewish Affairs that eventually ordered a census of all Jews. That census prepared the way for subsequent arrests, delivery to the German occupying forces, and deportation to the death camps. The question about religious affiliation on applications understandably made me nervous. The question also came up indirectly in ordinary conversations. Was it because of one's accent? People we met were almost inevitably curious. Where do you come from? Where were you born? Americans seemed to have an insatiable curiosity about origins and birthplaces.

There was an additional surprise. Most people we met, even some clearly Jewish, were reluctant to give credence or even to listen to stories we told of persecution in Europe. Hitler was bad, yes. But we must surely be exaggerating. What was the point of seeing only the dark side of things? What was the point of making waves? We should be grateful to find ourselves safe in the United States.

Behind my father's question about the presence of Jews on the Yale faculty I could sense an array of other questions—about me and my own attitude. He probably thought that up to a point I myself did not wish to make waves. He did not consider himself religious in any way, but he did have a strong sense of solidarity. He knew that someone born Black could not deny the inherited color, but that a person of Jewish background could pretend otherwise, could try disguising his family's identity, or use silence as a mask. For my father, there was shame in such denial. He knew from experience that anti-Semitism took many forms, but that it was all-pervasive, that the truth would eventually come out, and that there was dignity in not going into hiding.

The age-old prejudice remained alive even in a citadel of learning. It was noticeable in the reigning fashion of New Criticism. The literary idol was T. S. Eliot, whose poems and essays are peppered with disparaging remarks about Jews in modern society. In the teaching of English at Yale, it was easy to detect a not-so-hidden hostility toward the so-called group of New York intellectuals, largely made up of Jewish writers and scholars such as Alfred Kazin, Norman Podhoretz, Philip Rahv, and William Phillips, the editor of *Partisan Review*. The New Critics, who set the tone at Yale, chose to be attuned rather to the group of Southern Agrarians, whose leaders were John Crowe Ransom, Allen Tate, and Robert Penn Warren. The home of this group was Vanderbilt University; it was a group notorious for espousing conservative views, advocating traditional "values" as well as reverence for the past, and denouncing industrialization, the notion of progress, and the liberal views of the New York cultural establishment.

How ironic then that T. S. Eliot should have been so important in my early career. After only a couple of terms, I chose him as the subject of my senior thesis. It is true that I was quite taken with his poems about aging Prufrock and pub-haunting Sweeney. Not to mention the many voices, cosmopolitan allusions, and disturbing settings of *The Waste Land*, a poem that reminded me of my favorite French poet Charles Baudelaire. I remembered and recited to myself Eliot's striking lines the way one remembers snatches of songs and operatic arias—though there was nothing operatic about them. I delighted in images of "one-night cheap hotels" and evocations of "sawdust restaurants," their floors covered with oyster-shells. I had a distinct vision of the yellow fog rubbing its back in feline fashion against the windowpanes. I could literally see the "heap of broken images" in *The Waste Land*, the Dante-inspired crowds in the hell of the modern city. I was less enthralled by the philosophical pronouncements in *Four Quartets*, but nonetheless responded to the passage about being "distracted from distraction by distraction," which reminded me of Pascal's denunciation of divertissements, and above all, I appreciated the lines about the instability of language, about words that "slip, slide, perish" and are afflicted with imprecision—lines that I often recalled in the future as I struggled with words.

Why then did I not choose Eliot's poetry as the subject of my senior thesis, but rather his critical essays loaded with anti-liberal opinions endorsed with reverence by various members of the English department? And why did I choose to major in English, when my clear intention was to teach the gems of French literature?

The answer to the latter question is easy. It was the result of a most fortunate, unplanned encounter with a man who was to play a major role in my life: Henri Peyre. Soon after my arrival at Yale, I had climbed up the steep steps of William Harkness Hall to the third-floor offices of the French department to obtain information about course offerings. When the mild-spoken, fragile-looking faculty member whom I consulted became aware that I was interested in French literature as a professional career, he began listening to me with his mind evidently fixed on some higher region, and then uttered in hushed tones that he knew exactly the person I must, absolutely must, see. He pronounced the name of Henri Peyre with awe and an inspired look on his face. I still hear his words: "He is our great scholar, our great man." It was as though he were talking about a shaman, one capable of magically determining events. Peyre was obviously a legend, and not only on the Yale campus. I soon learned that he was far more than the chair of a prestigious department, he was a sort of cultural ambassador of France.

When I entered his monastic office, I was struck by the contrast between his expansiveness and the confined space he occupied. He teased me immediately about what he called my wartime "tourism" across combat zones, perilous adventures so unlike the life in an ivory tower that I now wished to inhabit. He teased me, but in a sunny, benign manner. He spoke with a stunning volubility, yet seemed to divine my questions and my wishes before I even had time to find my words. He was taking charge, outlining my curriculum, planning my future . . . and all the while answering the phone that kept ringing, rummaging through papers, jotting down notes. Never had I encountered such speed of thought and words, such mental agility, such immediate concern for another person. I came away from Peyre's office dizzy, but carrying with me the most precious advice: since I wanted to teach French literature, with which I was already somewhat familiar because of my lycée days in Paris, since moreover I intended to teach this literature in the United States, would it not be best, would it not be most reasonable to major in English before entering the French graduate department?

And this is how the veteran-novice came to be exposed to the *doxa* of New Criticism.

My family had mixed feelings about my career plans. Babushka, my lovable, imperious grandmother, deliberately misheard me whenever I referred to them. "So, you want to be a journalist," she would say, and this was already a comedown in her mind. Her engineer husband had helped develop the Russian railroads, then acquired a sugar refinery near Samara on the Volga. She spoke of relatives who were orchestra conductors or other celebrities, so she claimed—but never insignificant schoolteachers. She could recite lines from Pushkin, had set opinions, and would dictate to my mother who was socially acceptable and who was not. As for my quite bourgeois, well-to-do (thanks to an old family business) parents, they would gladly have seen me become a respected lawyer, an eminent surgeon, or even an opera singer (they idolized Chaliapin) provided I could make it to the top—so long as I did not consider a life in business. They had apparently chosen to forget that I had been a rather unmotivated lycée student, with typically frivolous adolescent interests. They had been informed on a number of occasions that I skipped school, though I never offered precise details about my delinquent activities. What I did on those occasions was to take the métro all by myself, emerge in some distant quarter of Paris, and relish feeling like a traveling explorer in a far-away region, among cityscapes of stone caressed by the mist so movingly evoked by Baudelaire. These walks in the perilously seductive modern city, these visions of the French poet's whorish metropolis, the "*énorme catin*," in turn, though much later, made me feel on quite familiar territory when I discovered T. S. Eliot at Yale and followed him through *The Waste Land*'s section on the "unreal city." The link between the two poets is in fact stressed by Eliot himself, who quotes Baudelaire's famous line that makes a hypocritical accomplice of the reader: "—Hypocrite lecteur,—mon semblable,—mon frère!"

Given my dilettantish Parisian studies, it still surprises me that I did so well at Yale when I returned from what my new mentor called "wartime tourism." After only one term and a summer program as freshman, I was promoted to junior year, and could thus complete my undergraduate work in just a little over two years. This promotion was based on my good grades at Yale and on work supposedly covered in the lycée. It explains how I miraculously avoided having to take any science courses. Which in turn explains why it was at all possible for me to end up with a 92 average, an academic honor of "Philosophical Orations," Yale's equivalent of summa cum laude, and a prize for my honors thesis consisting in its publication by Yale University Press. I would thus enter graduate school with a book already to my credit. If only my sponsors had known how indifferent, how inattentive a student I had been in my Parisian chemistry, physics, and mathematics classes! What redeems me somewhat in my own eyes, whenever I feel tempted to disparage retrospectively my youthful learning inclinations, is the recognition that I was passable in Latin (though frequently guilty of appalling solecisms and barbarisms), that history teachers held my attention, and that I loved to learn poetry by heart and delighted in impressing both class and teacher with my dramatic recitations. I still remember my histrionic triumph when I declaimed, during the politically troubled years of the late 1930s, André Chénier's poem written shortly before mounting the revolutionary scaffold to face the guillotine.

Still, my academic exploits in New Haven puzzle me today; I cannot get myself to take them seriously. Perhaps the sobering experience of war and the sense of having lost five years accounted for my new zeal. More than five years, in fact, if one begins with the day in 1940 when France was defeated, Marshal Pétain signed the humiliating armistice, and my studies were interrupted. My recent career resolve, as well as living off campus, explains why my college social life was unusually limited. I was in a hurry to make up for lost time. I also continued to see myself as a stranger. No fraternity, no secret society, no parties. After army life, I relished long hours of study and solitude. Only years later, when I had already joined the faculty, was I elected member of the Elizabethan Club and initiated, as an honorary fellow, into one of the societies, to the solemn chords of Mozart's *Magic Flute*—chords that more than ever seemed to be coming from another world.

THE IMPERSONAL THEORY OF POETRY

Bill Wimsatt's dismissive snorts when I first presented him with two summary pages of my project on T. S. Eliot had a galvanizing effect. I'll show him! According to Wimsatt, I was succumbing to the detestable biographical temptation, as well as to the "intentional fallacy," his bugbear. A double offense. When I returned to his office two days later, it was with a new summary statement, this time boldly confronting Eliot's critical essays, despite my distaste for his anti-liberal views and the pontifical solemnity to which he himself refers.

Again, the Jewish question. The anti-Semitic remarks in Eliot's poetry were unpalatable enough. In "Gerontion," the Jew squatting on the window sill—the owner of the "decayed house"—is said to have been "spawned" in an estaminet in Antwerp, a city known for its Jewish community engaged in the diamond trade. In another poem, a cigar-puffing Jew named Bleistein, a "Chicago Semite Viennese," is characterized by his saggy bent knees and "palms turned out," and associated with protozoic slime, rats, and "money in furs." As for the lowlife "silent vertebrate" (most likely a grasping prostitute) in one of the Sweeney poems, her identity is revealed in police-record style as Rachel née Rabinovitch. And there is more . . .

If one turns to Eliot's critical essays—admirable for his polished familiarity with the metaphysical poets Marvell and Donne, the Elizabethan theater, and writers as diverse as Baudelaire and Dante—they can easily indispose because of their sophistry, occasional priggishness, and underlying dogmatic views. When I now look, with a rearview-mirror perspective, at my decision to deal with Eliot's theoretical pronouncements, I marvel at my undergraduate eagerness to indulge in abstractions and "theory." Is this the same person who years later felt so disturbed when his own graduate students were mesmerized by imported postmodern theories to the point of no longer enjoying literature? The truth is that at the time I was impressed by Eliot's famous essay "Tradition and the Individual Talent," and by the formulaic doctrines of the New Critics.

But what exactly, I now ask myself, is this "impersonal theory" of poetry? I search for help in my slim book which came out shortly after my graduation in a printing of five hundred copies, as a prize for my senior essay. As I now reread this published honors" thesis, I gather that Eliot's theory can be summed up by a few questionable statements: that the difference between art and life's events is always absolute, that art is an end in itself, that the poet is only a medium and must aim at the extinction of his personality, that poetry is not the expression of a subjectivity but an escape from it. It follows, according to Eliot, that the critic also must avoid expressing any private emotions. I now wonder why I would spend time on similar asseverations when I knew even then that great literature is not mere rhetoric but that it deals with issues of life and death, and how to face our mortal condition.

It is clear that in my senior year I was already skeptical about the validity of some of Eliot's central arguments. It did not take me long to express my misgivings and objections more fully once I felt liberated from the major tenets of New Criticism, especially after beginning graduate studies in French, and later joining their faculty. And more than liberated. For the recently launched *Yale French Studies* I wrote an essay entitled "T. S. Eliot and the Romantic Heresy," in which I vented my accumulated misgivings and resentments, intensified, no doubt, by my growing fondness for the Romantic period which Eliot treats with such disdain. My irritation was further fueled by the devious ways in which

Eliot, while pretending to banish concern for beliefs from the study of literature, surreptitiously and persistently introduces Christian themes, with recourse to loaded terms such as "orthodoxy," "heterodoxy," and "heresy"—terms giving off strong whiffs of dogma, inquisition, and excommunication. *A Primer in Heresy* is in fact the subtitle of a book in which Eliot denounces a society worm-eaten with liberalism, proclaiming the undesirability of freethinking Jews and revealing an affinity with other reactionary detractors of modern civilization. He openly expressed his admiration for Charles Maurras, extreme right-wing apostle of order and tradition, self-proclaimed enemy of the idea of progress, and inspirational force behind French anti-Semitism at the time.

As a novice to formal literary studies, I was attracted (for a while) to a purist notion of the perfectly crafted work of art. The image of the "well-wrought urn," made famous by the title of one of Cleanth Brooks's books, had become emblematic of the aesthetic credo of Yale's English department. Temporary devotion to this purist ideal may account for my partial blindness to the less attractive features of Eliot's work. The French department helped enlighten me. The nostalgic reactionary Charles Maurras was not a hero there. Collectively and individually, the French faculty was committed to an eclectic view of history. Dogmatic, ahistorical readings of literature made no sense in the context of rapid and disruptive successions of French political regimes that often rendered difficult the dialogue between father and son, even between brother and brother: the Ancien Régime, the Revolution, the Directory and the Consulate, the Napoleonic epoch, the Restoration, the July Monarchy, the Second Empire, the Third Republic—and then the defeat of 1940, the Occupation and Vichy, and more recently the era of Charles de Gaulle . . .

Not only were historical considerations omnipresent in French literary studies, but biography—held to be irrelevant by Wimsatt and his followers—was considered essential to the understanding of an author's works. "L'homme et l'œuvre"—the writer and his work—was the subtitle of many a monograph. Which meant that hardly any detail of a writer's life was deemed unimportant to an understanding of the author's work. Such a notion, inviting anecdotal approaches, could of course also be carried to unwelcome extremes.

A paper of mine on Albert Camus had drawn the attention of Henri Peyre, who recommended it for publication. The Peyre course for which

it had been written was on the modern French novel and theater—a dazzling course extending well beyond the borders of France. We knew that
our professor had made his reputation with a book on the French classical period of the seventeenth century, the period of Louis XIV and the
court of Versailles. But we quickly sensed that he also had a passionate
and extensive expertise in the arts of the twentieth century, and the various manifestations of modernity. Proust, Picasso, Stravinsky were pivotal figures, but they were hardly alone. The cultural scene was crowded
with original talents and with rebellious groups and movements such as
Dada and Surrealism. The pervasive sense of crisis and discontinuities
before and after World War I favored experimentation in the novel, often influenced by cinematographic techniques, while the theater, facing
an increasingly heterogeneous public, tested new forms and new meth-
ods. In Peyre's class we learned about innovative Parisian stage directors
such as Jacques Copeau, Gaston Baty, Charles Dullin, Georges Pitoëff,
Louis Jouvet, and others, who had produced works by Ibsen, Chekhov,
Pirandello, Schnitzler, Giraudoux, and Cocteau. It was a heady scene,
and those distant whiffs from the Parisian avant-garde were a whole lot
more exciting, it seemed to me, than what was going on in England at
the time—and by extension in the English department.

Yet I still had one foot in the English department, and was even invited to participate in a program conceived and directed by one of their
celebrities. Again between two worlds.

3 · What Existentialism Meant to Us

One day, during my junior year, two advanced graduate students, Bob Cohn and Ted Morris, chief instigators of the first issue of *Yale French Studies*, knocked on my door, sat down, one on the bed, the other on my only chair, and asked me point-blank about whether I would be willing to contribute a paper I had written on Albert Camus to the inaugural issue devoted to Existentialism. I was, needless to say, taken aback and immensely flattered. As an undergraduate, I was aware of my two visitors' prestige as prize graduate students. Bob Cohn promised to become the expert interpreter of Stéphane Mallarmé; and Ted Morris, passionate about the French avant-garde, was already something of an authority on Alfred Jarry, the creator of king Ubu, the wildly grotesque protagonist of the play *Ubu roi*.

It was evidently Henri Peyre, for whose class I had written on Camus's *L'Étranger* (*The Stranger*), who had recommended that Ted and Bob pay me a visit. The essay did indeed appear in the first issue of *Yale French Studies*. It was my first publication and I felt quite proud at the time, although I have almost come to regret this early appearance in print, somewhat embarrassed by what I soon came to consider the wrongheadedness of some of my remarks.

Peyre's course was dazzling. It extended well beyond the borders of France and covered various manifestations of modernity. His lectures were a steady elation. We delighted in his mellifluous voice and exhilarating presentations. We loved his surprising digressions as he swiftly moved from Greek mythology to Tolstoy's musings on mortality, from the Hellenism of Renan to the political theories of Machiavelli, from Baudelaire's reveries as flâneur to the brutalities of political repression.

Among the first to sense the full significance of Existentialism in the recent historical and political context, Peyre stressed the moral dilemmas experienced in France during the Occupation. The very title of Simone de Beauvoir's novel *Le sang des autres* (*The Blood of Others*) points to the anguishing question of whether a Resistance fighter, having freely chosen the path of heroic self-sacrifice, has the moral right to risk by his actions the lives of others who have not made a similar choice. The problem of choice and freedom is at the heart of the novel. It is even more pointedly so in Jean-Paul Sartre's *Les mouches* (*The Flies*), written during the Occupation, when questions of freedom had multiple resonances. The play deals transparently with the themes of bad conscience and oppressive guilt associated with the festering wound of the Vichy regime and collaboration with the Nazis.

Sartre was at the center of our discussions. We had also read his prewar novel *La nausée* (*Nausea*), struck by its sense of immediacy. But what exactly did Sartre mean to us? He was a philosophy teacher, yet he refused to play the traditional role of guide and model—of "maître à penser." He brought philosophy out of the classroom into our daily acts and behavior. We could not light a cigarette, pour a glass of whiskey, or listen to our favorite jazz without raising big questions. No activity, no gesture, was innocent of meaning. Sartre alerted us to our bad faith, to the traps of inauthenticity, to the lies with which we choose to live. He made philosophy as immediate as our daily moves, and our thoughts as fascinating to us as the enlarged figures on a movie screen. We felt a strange, almost welcome anguish in this self-consciousness, and there was poetry in it, too. Everything seemed new again in a way that was quite different from the newness offered by an André Gide or the Surrealists. What this physically unattractive man meant to many of us was the almost impossible attempt to live without morally cheating. Sartre taught us that neither language nor silence is without meaning; that whatever we say, or fail to say, creates or negates values; that every act, as well as every refusal to act, betrays a project.

We learned from Sartre above all that the function of literature was to make society feel guilty and to disrupt the agenda of conservative forces. His views were made explicit in the essay "What is Literature?" (1948), which we had no trouble setting against the background of the ominous prewar years, followed by the Nazi occupation of France. Two major collective experiences account for the climate in which the sensibility and the ideas of Sartre could develop. The first is the seemingly endless political crisis of the 1930s during which I myself grew up: the economic depression, the rise of fascism and Nazism, the spreading horror of concentration camps, the shame of appeasement—a period that thrust Europe into history-as-nightmare, making intellectuals like Sartre aware that this was no longer a time to seek private salvation through art, that private salvation was in fact impossible, that all of us are involved in a collective tragedy, and that the very meaning of traditional humanism has to be challenged.

The second major experience was the 1940 invasion and occupation of France by the Germans, a period of humiliation and betrayal, but one that also offered singular opportunities for moral choices and for courage—a period when deportation to extermination camps, execution of hostages, and torture by the Gestapo became daily realities, when human beings were daily exposed to extreme situations, and ethical problems could not be comfortably relegated to the classroom but had to be faced here and now, leaving little room for cozy abstractions.

Torture, especially, was a haunting subject for Sartre. The Nazi atrocities at Dachau and Auschwitz were for him not merely a cause for moral indignation, but a steady sense of guilt. He insisted on remembering the atmosphere of culpability during the Occupation when human beings were degraded and destroyed while others were eating, sleeping, or making love. Mental pictures such as these made vivid for him the unbreachable gap between the victim and the well-meaning conscience that speaks up on its behalf. We understood, though vaguely, that this precisely was the basic drama of the modern intellectual who feels compelled to speak up for the victims, while feeling unsure about having the right to speak on their behalf. For where is his mandate, not having himself also suffered in the flesh, and known fully the extremes of abjections?

Many of my generation felt drawn to this exalted sense of guilt. We liked to quote a sentence from Dostoevsky: "Everybody is responsible to everybody for everything." When Sartre's brand of existentialism reached us, it opened up a period of intellectual fervor. As we read his novel in diary form, *La nausée*, we experienced a sense of discontinuity in a permanently fragmented present. We were initiated to a sense of alienation, to the narrator's mirror-disease of thinking. We were thrilled to discover, together with the protagonist of this antinovel, that life has no fanfare beginnings and no fanfare ends. But tragic lucidity does not

lead to despair. We understood the lesson imparted. Since life has no inherent meaning, the only meaning it can have is the meaning we give to
it. The absence of meaning condemns us to freedom, and this freedom
in turn condemns us to responsibility, to being *engagé*. Every heartbeat,
we learned, thrusts into the world a decision not to be recalled. Every act
means a choice, even silence and the choice not to act.

The political implications were obvious, as was made clear in Sartre's
play *Les mouches* (*The Flies*), performed in 1943 under the German occupation, at a time when the word and concept of freedom were loaded with
tragic potential. Sartre made use of the ancient Greek myth that Aeschylus
had dramatized in *The Oresteia* but gives it a new twist. His Orestes commits his irrevocable crime in order to share the guilt of the city of Argos.
It was impossible not to see a striking parallel between Sartre's Argos and
the France under the Nazis and the Vichy régime of Marshal Pétain—a
France defeated, guilt-ridden, and degradingly submissive to its rulers.
The play is studded with topical allusions. The tyrants keep collective re-
morse alive, just as in France, after the defeat of 1940, the Vichy govern-
ment fostered a climate of mea culpa breast-beating, and this not only as
a means of discrediting the defunct Third Republic, but so as to promote
the proper spirit of atonement and submissiveness. King Aegisthus and
Pétain are both collaborators. Pétain collaborates with the Nazi tyranny,
and Aegisthus collaborates with the tyranny of Zeus. As we read the play,
we were transfixed by the political allegory that allowed for no escape
from moral and political responsibility.

And then there was Sartre's way of expressing himself. His language
suggested the viscous quality of existence, the proliferation of things, in
accents and rhythms that sounded new to us. His was a pungent, acrid
style that blended the colloquial with the abstract, a style that unmasked
the lies of received opinions, a style we liked because it seemed to carry
the smell of bistros and Gauloises cigarettes, the emanations of the Paris
métro, the smoky warmth of the Café Les Deux Magots where he and
his friends and admirers gathered, and that became a place of pilgrim-
age in the postwar years.

•   •   •

Sartre and Simone de Beauvoir were not the only exalted figures during
the so-called Existentialist period. Albert Camus was another revered

literary celebrity. I felt especially drawn to him. He was often associated with the Existentialist group, largely because he developed the theme of the "absurd" in *Le mythe de Sisyphe* (*The Myth of Sisyphus*). This association, however, was questionable. He had been on friendly terms with Sartre, but ideological differences soon led to a harsh public quarrel. When I later read *La chute* (*The Fall*), I admired the bitter irony of its duplicitous fictional narrator, whose hyperlucid voice, coming from a Dostoevskyan underground, deconstructs the Parisian intellectual establishment ruled by Sartre and his acolytes.

That dominance was in the end ephemeral. It is Camus's voice, decades later, that is still heard. Temperamentally not drawn to abstractions, Camus is truest to himself when surrendering to the sensuous and the poetic, to the bittersweet awareness of the fragile beauties of this world, which according to him is our only kingdom. He turned against the intellectual gurus of the Parisian scene who occupied center stage in the late 1940s and 1950s because he concluded that they were accomplices of the lethal microbe of intransigent ideologies, and preaching in a spiritual desert.

Yale's French department was largely responsible for the sudden excitement about Existentialism in American universities. But *Yale French Studies*, with its initial issue on Existentialism, could not have come into being without the encouragement, support, and inspiring presence of Henri Peyre. Only when I myself became a member of the faculty did I fully realize to what extent he had shaped the department. He had surrounded himself with a devoted junior group. We felt protected and stimulated by his scintillating personality. For twenty-five years he presided, unrivaled and unchallenged, over the destiny of the department. Those years—the Peyre years—were also, largely because of his radiant presence, the golden years of French studies in this country. Hardly any French celebrity crossed the ocean without an obligatory visit to Yale.

Peyre was a mentor and a model. We admired his sparkle and energy, his generosity, his erudition and feats of memory, his teaching a full schedule while chairing a large department, remaining active on several national committees, and publishing one book after another. At departmental meetings, which he chaired in presidential style, he gave stunning performances. For two full hours, he provided overviews and analyses, answered questions no one had asked, gave ample credit to all concerned, listing articles, books, and honors accrued. He never mentioned his own achievements, but he did occupy center stage for the duration of the meeting. He covered all the activities (including theatrical) of the department, explained, reminisced, amused, teased, announced new appointments as well as the arrival of visiting professors—all this in firework sentences, studded with digressions and subordinate clauses, that were unfailingly completed and would fall back on their feet with acrobatic agility. No wonder that when the time came, I faced the news of my appointment as the next department chair with disbelief and anxiety.

Peyre had greatly encouraged me when I planned to write a book on the role of intellectuals in the modern French novel in which Sartre, Malraux, Camus, Simone de Beauvoir, and Louis Guilloux were to play prominent roles. The Existentialist moment had clearly left its mark on me. Years after I published *The Intellectual Hero*, and the existentialist fever had subsided, I returned once more to Sartre, even though I had come to recognize his ideological excesses. The occasion was a 1972 invitation to offer a seminar at the Scuola Normale in Pisa. A recent publishing event determined my choice of subject. Sartre's *L'Idiot de la famille* (*The Family Idiot*) had just appeared—an unwieldy study of Flaubert, over two thousand pages of existentialist psychoanalysis filled with arbitrary hypotheses and reductive conclusions fictionalizing relations of the young Gustave with his family, but containing new and provocative insights, especially about the writer's formative years and his juvenile writings. Sartre saw Gustave as oppressed and repressed by the crushing presence of his father, the domineering chief surgeon at Rouen's Hôtel-Dieu hospital, and living out the rest of his life in a state of permanent resentment. Hatred of the father, according to Sartre, translated into hatred of life. Early epilepsy served as an alibi for refusing to pursue a career, for seeking refuge in a radical passivity and in the religion of art. Sartre's Flaubert thus regards himself as already posthumous, as having joined the invisible community of great artists. It was an old Sartrean theme, a censure previously directed against Baudelaire and others—writers who saw themselves as already dead while still alive.

This censure also points to a capital existentialist lesson. Every escape into the cult of "essence" and of "being" is to be repudiated because it is a denial and betrayal of becoming and human responsibility, and thus a refusal to be morally committed to the ever pressing and unpredictable present—a commitment that stands as a fundamental credo of Existentialism.

4 · Cleopatra at Yale

Shakespeare's Iago had already disturbed some of my students. Why was he so mean? They could not accept pure and simple evil. There must be a reason, a cause for his nastiness. Soon after, we were reading *Antony and Cleopatra*, and some of the all-male students could not make sense of the Egyptian queen. (This was some years before women were admitted.) Was she a "triple-turn'd whore," as Antony calls her in a moment of burning anger, feeling betrayed? In the first scene of the play, Philo refers to her as a "strumpet." So why did the holy priests bless her when she was "riggish," my students asked? And when she later proclaims that she is now "marble constant," no longer fickle and treacherous, that she now has "nothing of woman" in her—was that not, my undergraduates asked, a demeaning thing to say regarding her own sex?

These questions came from students in a collectively taught program, Directed Studies—a program for selected undergraduates, combining studies in literature, philosophy, and history of arts. The young men's uneasiness in my seminar with the figure of Cleopatra determined the theme of the lecture I was assigned to give to the assembled group of over one hundred freshmen sometime in the late 1950s. Recently going through some hidden folders, I came across faded pages of notes for this lecture. I don't recall whether I consulted any commentaries on the play. Certainly, I was in no way a Shakespeare scholar. But I loved the play; it spoke to me at some deep level. I may have benefited from the Shakespeare expertise of Maynard Mack, who directed our program. And I surely discussed the play with my admired friend Bernard Knox, the great classical scholar, who had been a stellar presence in the program.

On rereading my old lecture notes, it became apparent that my students' perplexities about the inconsistencies of Cleopatra's character lay behind my decision to stress, in my seminar as well as in the lecture to the entire group, the redemptive nature of the play's final act. I knew that some of my students almost considered that last act as superfluous and wordy. For what more could happen after the end of act 4? Antony is dead by now, his power gone. The irreplaceable is lost, the past now irretrievable. Cleopatra, we know, must also die. We even know how she will die. It's all in Plutarch, and probably in the program notes. And if the performance was successful, we have been so moved by the autumnal beauty of the ultimate scene of the fourth act—the love scene in the symbolic monument—so carried away by the golden moment, by the final words of dying Antony and the courageously smiling Cleopatra (smiling, as it were, at grief) that for us also there seems to be nothing remarkable left beneath the visiting moon. We too, echoing Cleopatra, may feel that "the lamp is spent," that there is hardly any point to abiding in a dull and empty world.

Some students in my discussion group, looking back to our own readings of classical plays earlier in the course, observed that if *Antony and Cleopatra* came to an end with act 4, it would still deserve its reputation as one of the most dramatic and sensuous theatrical experiences in the Western tradition. In some of the famous tragedies, sex appears as a raw, vital force. Clytemnestra, in Aeschylus's *Agamemnon*, savors murder as a sexual ritual, comparing herself to a garden fertilized by her husband's gushing blood as by springtime showers. The murder of Cassandra, so Clytemnestra also claims, has given new excitement to her bed's delights with her lover Aegisthus. In Shakespeare's *Othello*, Iago's obscene zoological lexicon—about old black rams, white ewes, Barbary horses, beasts with two backs—serves to provoke the sexual jealousy of the Moor, and as a demonic corrosion of innocence. And in *King Lear*, violence and lechery inform a bestial natural world where flies and horses go to it pell-mell, where copulation thrives, and sex seems altogether repulsive.

How totally different, I pointed out to my group, are the references to sexuality in *Antony and Cleopatra*. Lovemaking takes the form of a joyful sport, an imaginative urge to manifest character and vitality! It appears as the very meaning of life. "The nobleness of life is to do thus," says Antony. Physical love is here surrounded and heightened by elegance, luxury, and artifice. It may be a force of nature, as suggested by insistent references to fertility and to the river Nile; but the verbal imagery repeatedly raises sex to a level of refined eroticism. "O happy horse to bear the weight of Antony," exclaims Cleopatra in a longing mood (though I wondered whether women students, if admitted to our program, would appreciate the playful equine imagery). This playful sexuality is a significant feature of the first acts. Cleopatra's way of loving is compared to a sophisticated gastronomic experience, to a delicate Epicurean feast that sharpens the appetite with a provocative sauce and renews the appetite at the very moment of satisfaction: "She makes hungry where most she satisfies," explains Enobarbus.

Carnal relations are elevated to an artistic level. For eroticism stimulates the powers of the imagination, intensifying both the anticipated and the recollected moment, creating a sense of time that, within the dramatic progression of the play, conveys a nostalgia for what is lost, or about to be lost. Even though artfully stimulated and stimulating, this is not a frivolous sexuality, but one that almost borders on a transcendent experience. Enobarbus, the lucid observer, remarks early in the play that the vilest things are becoming in Cleopatra, that the holy priests bless her when she is "riggish"—namely wanton, lustful, bawdy. (I glossed the adjective "riggish," and its significance in the context.) Cleopatra herself, one might say, is the high priestess of a cult that, like all true cults, demands ultimate sacrifices made with abnegation and joy.

Antony's radiant words, as he is brought dying to Cleopatra's monument, bear witness to this exaltation of the senses: "Of many thousand kisses the poor last / I lay upon thy lips."

Cleopatra's character, my Yalies agreed, displays variations on the theme of caprice and fickleness. Yet her ability to put on at will the masks of sadness or gaiety reveals something beyond the perverse talent of a "false soul" (as Antony refers to her at the height of his anger at her apparent betrayal). Her histrionic versatility also manifests the deeper urge to transcend the ordinary conditions of life by means of any rapture—be it the passion of play, intoxication with the power of her own attractiveness, the amorous state, and even the exultation of a freely chosen death. The ecstatic moment has as its counterpart that "gap of time" afflicting Cleopatra when she is depressed, as during Antony's prolonged absence: "Give me to drink mandragora . . . / That I might sleep out this great gap of time."

Antony himself offers the paradox of an apparent moral degradation that in the end is nothing of the sort. For this "strumpet's fool" (as he is described in the opening moments of the play), who is later seen as having given up an empire for a foreign seductress, this heroic figure who was once, though daintily brought up, a tough soldier capable under duress of drinking the urine of horses, is now seemingly undermined by voluptuary Egypt and the aphrodisiac charms of its lascivious queen. Yet in the face of defeat, he displays a courage and nobility that may appear as an impetuous last fling at destiny, but in reality is a defiance of death by means of a lover's loyalty that even death cannot deny. Mutability and treason, whether in the form of a lustful queen or in that of a brave soldier named Enobarbus, seem powerless in the end against the stronger example of constancy and fidelity. Nothing could be more moving than Antony's calm words after he discovers that he has mortally wounded himself on the basis of a deception: "Bear me, good friends, where Cleopatra bides."

Even if *Antony and Cleopatra* ended with act 4, we agreed that the play would still give satisfying developments to major themes. The political satire is brought to a head in the masterful scene on Pompey's galley with its caricature of worldly power in the form of the triumvirs' drunken dance and song—a satire that helps discredit those very Roman values that lead to a Roman victory. But this victory is hardly a victory. Shakespeare's poetic voice steadily reaffirms a longing for the values betrayed in the uneven struggle between the power of the personality and the frigid impersonality of power.

Even the tragic sense might be partially satisfied by the time we reach the end of act 4. Cleopatra has learned to be almost humble in her newly discovered humanity. Addressed as "Royal Egypt!" and "Empress!" by her loyal attendants, she responds:

> No more, but e'en a woman, and commanded
> By such poor passion as the maid that milks
> And does the meanest chores.

As the fourth act draws to a close, she has acquired that cruel lucidity which impels the traditional tragic hero (a central theme in our course) to stare into the unadorned face of destiny. "All strange and terrible events are welcome, / But comforts we despise."

• • •

Many themes appear successfully treated in the first four acts: tragic
clairvoyance, refined eroticism, existential fear of time, the interplay
of permanence and change, nostalgia for the values of the personality. Yet I was eager to reach our discussion of the final act, which marks
not merely a prolonged suspension between the regretted past and
Cleopatra's self-willed death and great last sleep. It is the telling dramatic space where a transient human experience is translated into a new
state of immutability—and this before the fact of Cleopatra's death, as
though the dream could precede the slumber.

Lyrical verses stud this transforming final act: Octavius Caesar's lament over the demise of his "mate in empire"; Cleopatra's evocation
of the man whose raised arm crested the world, whose delights were
"dolphin-like"; her yearning for sleep and imagined departure in her regal attire for another Cydnus; her longing as she applies the deadly asp
to her breast, comparing it to a baby that sucks its nurse asleep; Octavius
Caesar's entranced words as he contemplates the dead queen:

> She looks like sleep,
> As she would catch another Antony
> In her strong toil of grace

Remarkably, nearly all these poetic passages follow a similar pattern.
They are concerned both with the past and with the desired sleep. Shakespeare even treats this sleep motif ironically. (Irony and lyricism can
paradoxically cohabit, as I did my best to explain.) Trying to comfort
Cleopatra, victorious Octavius Caesar advises her to "feed, and sleep."
But the deeper meaning of sleep cannot escape. "O! such another sleep
that I might see / But such another man." There is, however, not a trace
of irony in Cleopatra's death wish. Sleep serves here as a symbol by
means of which death and memory are interwoven, inducing us to consider the fleetingness of a necessarily imperfect human experience from
the viewpoint of the timeless. Act 5 marks the intrusion of the atemporal
into the world of time and change.

Although this ultimate act seems to be centered on Cleopatra, its
true significance, as some alert students observed, extends well beyond

her. The beauty of its most memorable lines is melancholy, a prolonged
melodious echo of the dying strains of the previous act, now transposed
onto a higher level and into another key. Speculations on the mystery
of Cleopatra's character were of little help in accounting for this new
mood. What is she really? When is she sincere? What are her motives? Is
she a royal harlot? These were some of the questions raised in the Yale
classroom. Since she has determined to die, why does she send a mes-
senger to Octavius Caesar? Why kneel to this future emperor and call
him master and lord? Does she wish to fool him? Does she offer herself
to him? Or is it that she cannot help playacting, cannot help betraying
Antony—even after his death? Or is it that deceit and artifice are now
made to serve new resolutions? The mystery of Cleopatra's being would
seem to lead to a broader mystery.

Nor did it help to consider her as a force of nature, inexplicable yet recurring, like the timeless cycles of the seasons and the swelling of the river
Nile. Enobarbus says that age cannot wither her. She herself talks of being
"wrinkled deep in time." Repeatedly, she is compared to the great river
and to the earth of Egypt. Yet Cleopatra cannot be equated with "nature,"
or what is natural. In more ways than one, she represents a force outside
of nature, or even in conflict with nature, outwitting and dominating it.

This insubordination to nature is the underlying theme of Enobarbus's
already mentioned description:

> Age cannot wither her, nor custom stale
> Her infinite variety; other women cloy
> The appetites they feed, but she makes hungry
> Where most she satisfies; for vilest things
> Become themselves in her, that the holy priests
> Bless her when she is riggish.

The entire passage sets Cleopatra outside and above the natural order
of things. She is not subject to the laws of time and decay (age cannot wither her), and in her sexual being she stands in stark contrast to
other women, as though in denial of the laws of nature. Her vilest actions and most wanton behavior are transmuted into something rich and
rare—something almost sacred. The priests' blessing of her lustfulness
appears like a hieratic consecration. (This my young all-male undergraduates had some trouble accepting.)

I kept insisting that Enobarbus's mesmerizing account of Cleopatra's arrival on the river Cydnus reinforces this sense of a dominance over nature. The burnished throne, the golden poop of her boat, the silver oars, her accoutrements, the ambient perfume wafting around smiling cupids and attendant mermaids, all create an atmosphere of art and artifice in which nature is subdued, even denied, to the point where winds become lovesick with the fragrance, and the water falls in love with the stroke of the oars. Cleopatra herself is explicitly depicted as doubly superior to nature for she outdoes the painting of Venus, which is itself a work in which fancy can be seen to "outwork nature." Antony also, especially in Cleopatra's memory, appears superior to the ordinary laws and limitations of nature. She remembers that there was no winter to his bounty, that it was an autumn that grew the more by reaping (the imagery negates the seasons and the life/death cycle), that his delights were "dolphin-like," displaying his back above the elements he inhabited. Here again, negation of the natural rhythm is linked to a sense of elevation and spiritual freedom.

It is Cleopatra, however, who remains the principal embodiment of the conflict between nature and artifice. She herself seems to be a work of art. Enobarbus makes this point, only half in jest, at the beginning of the play, when he refers to her as a "wonderful piece of work." A work of artifice, one should add, not a work of nature—or rather a work in which artifice serves as a liberation from the constraining laws of nature, and ultimately as a liberation from her own flaws. And this with keen self-awareness, for it is at the very instant she playacts once again, putting on her regal robe and crown in preparation for a well-planned and well-staged death scene, that she asserts: "I am fire and air; my other elements / I give to baser life."

Artifice is inseparable from theatricality. Cleopatra loves to roam the streets of Alexandria in disguise, and Antony indulges in histrionics to make his followers weep as though they were spectators at a tragic performance. Even when they seem to behave most passionately, the protagonists are putting on an act for others and for themselves. Cleopatra's very first line has a theatrical ring to it. "If it be love indeed, tell me how much." One can hardly speak of a single intimate love scene between them. At no point in the play, not even when they sound most emotional or lyrical, do they find themselves alone with each other, without witnesses.

Playacting and references to playacting pervade Shakespeare's trag-edy, frequently carrying a symbolic significance. One of Cleopatra's favorite impersonations is the Egyptian goddess Isis, who represents the female principle reputed to have magical powers over fate itself and is also associated with flood and the moon—a goddess of fertil-ity and change, capable of assuming all manner of shapes and guises. References to the moon recur at key moments in the text.

Shakespeare's Cleopatra would seem to embody the interplay be-tween nature and artifice. Above and beyond her natural attractiveness, she attains true beauty by means of artful ingenuity, just as the artist, far from imitating nature, is substantially in revolt against it, and this precisely through his "art," which, even etymologically, is related to artifice—namely contrivance, device, even duplicity. At this point in the discussion, I could not resist drawing on my French connection.

In his provocative essay "Éloge du maquillage" (In Praise of Makeup), Charles Baudelaire remarked that beauty, like virtue, was an artificial product of the human mind. Cleopatra's and Antony's fondness for what they call "sport" must be understood in just such a way. For sport, like any game, or art itself (including the writing of a play), requires its own rules and imposes its own order.

Antony's urge to celebrate on the eve of his defeat can be considered in the same perspective: "Let's have one other gaudy night . . . let's mock the midnight bell." The verb "mock" in relation to the hour of mid-night clearly expresses the desire to defy the natural flow of time and achieve a liberation from normal constraints. Death itself is ultimately mocked and cheated, as fancy outwits nature by means of the least natu-ral of deaths, namely suicide. And there is a double trickery involved. Antony's self-willed death is the result of a deception, and this is even truer of Cleopatra's death characterized by a supreme form of artifice. For nature (the deadly asp) is used against nature as the queen know-ingly, and with clever refinements, prepares and enacts self-murder as one of the fine arts.

The central message of the all-important last act extends well beyond the destiny of individual characters. "The death of Antony is not a single doom," says Octavius Caesar. But neither are Cleopatra's life, love, and death a single doom. And just as the protagonists cannot be properly dis-cussed in isolation, so also this final act functions in relation, and also in opposition, to what precedes it. The ultimate scenes are conceived in such a manner as to induce the spectator or reader into a revision of the whole. This entire act without Antony imposes a very special awareness of the past, as well as a sense of time. These are at the center of Cleopatra's memory but have equally become our memory, our sense of time, within the theatrical or reading experience.

Even the smallest details of the previous acts acquire a new, sometimes ironic, but always enriched value when judged with hindsight. How convincing Philo sounds in the first scene of the play, when he announces that Antony, the "triple pillar of the world," has been turned into a "strumpet's fool"—a view shared by a few of my macho freshmen. Yet how foolish himself, how unjust and mistaken Philo shows himself to be, if one considers that the one truth the play makes clear is that Cleopatra is far indeed from an ordinary strumpet, and Antony very far from being a fool. Many remarks and images similarly take on a different meaning in retrospect.

Cleopatra, in the first scene, asks teasingly, "If it be love indeed, tell me how much." Antony's death—but much later—provides the answer. When Cleopatra proudly affirms, again in the first scene, that it is she who will "set a bourn" to how far to be loved, Antony answers on the same playful note that she will have to discover new heaven and new earth. But does this not turn out at the end to be profoundly true? I asked— Does their love not lead them to the discovery of previously unknown regions of the spirit? Again in the same first scene, when Antony kisses Cleopatra and states that "the nobleness of life is to do thus," his words may sound somewhat frivolous—a misuse of the word "nobleness." Yet by the time we read act 5, are we still convinced that the ways of Egypt are inferior to those of Rome? Are we still so sure that a love such as theirs, binding two human beings in intense pleasure and in death, is not perhaps the only truly worthwhile "nobleness" of life? "Kingdoms are clay," proclaims Antony defiantly in the first scene. Coming from a Roman triumvir, this utterance sounds irresponsible. Yet is it not also profoundly true, if one considers the historical ebb and flow of political power, often in decline at the very moment of apparent victory?

And there is more. When Enobarbus jokingly comments on Cleopatra's "celerity in dying," this is not only an allusion to her theatricality and lasciviousness ("dying" having a double meaning in Elizabethan parlance, as I saw fit to remind the class); Enobarbus's witticism proves to be ironically prophetic. Serpents and poisons are mentioned a number of times, usually in relation to each other, and both in relation to Cleopatra (who is lovingly called by Antony "serpent of old Nile")—clear evidence that Shakespeare planted these references early in the play with the snakebite suicide of the end in mind. At the conclusion of the first act, Cleopatra asks for a drink of mandragora so she may sleep out "the great gap of time" her Antony is far away. Once we have reached the final act, it is impossible not to establish a symbolic link with her death wish, also expressed in terms of a yearning for sleep.

The subject of death occasions the largest number of foreshadowing signals. Readying himself for the ultimate battle with Octavius Caesar, Antony defiantly declares, "I'll make Death love me." Love and death are of course coupled in the scene inside the monument, but in a manner Antony could not possibly have foreseen. He calls the Egyptian queen the armorer of his heart. She does indeed lovingly help him put on his armor, but her real effect on him is not through this kind of armoring, just as Antony's real strength manifests itself ultimately not on the battlefield. The false news of Cleopatra's death is more ironic still. Not only does her pretended death provoke Antony's real death (which in turn provokes Cleopatra's suicide), but revealing echoes help transform the false news into a lasting truth. According to the false report, her last words before dying are reported to have been "Antony, my noble Antony!" But those are about the exact same words ("O Antony!") she really pronounces as she applies another asp to her arm. An even more telling example of such revelatory echoes is provided by Antony's exclamation as he decides to throw himself on his sword after hearing the false news of Cleopatra's death ("I come, my queen")—words that Cleopatra almost literally repeats, as she is about to apply the asp to her breast: "Husband, I come."

· · ·

Just as earlier details in the tragedy foreshadow, often in an ironic mode, some of the telling developments of act 5, so this last act is in turn suffused with echoes of past moments, while transforming the significance of the previous verbal imagery. As Cleopatra prepares for the snake's bite, she asks to be dressed in her finest attire and imagines that she is once more to meet Antony on the river Cydnus. "Show me, my women, like a Queen. I am again for Cydnus." Why Cydnus?, students asked.

Is it mere melodramatic daydreaming and self-indulgent nostalgia? Cydnus is of course the place of the first and determining encounter with Antony, when Cleopatra, in festive fluvial procession, appeared like a reincarnation of Venus setting out to meet a god. That first meeting at Cydnus marks the beginning of their love affair in the world of time and change. But this new, imaginary journey of the final act conveys far more than the sentimental desire to recapture fleeting moments of a precious past. It expresses, without having to state it, the longing to join her lover for a final reunion in death, in the world of permanent forms.

"Give me my robe, put on my crown; I have / Immortal longings in me," says Cleopatra as she prepares for this final encounter. In experiencing death as a love act, she embodies the age-old coupling of love and death. Suspended between two self-inflicted deaths, the four hundred and fifty lines of the last act could be considered poetic variations on death as an erotic and aesthetic experience, and above all as a victory over mortality.

The association of eroticism with death is not new in Western literature. Here I turned somewhat pedantic, explaining that the *Liebestod*, the spiritual union of lovers in death, their attraction to death as a yearning for total love, appears in medieval and Renaissance texts well before Richard Wagner gave it perhaps its most moving expression in *Tristan und Isolde*. *Amour* and *mort*: French poets are fond of playing with these two words that sound alike. Shakespeare's Romeo, about to take his own life, descends to Juliet's tomb, calling it "this bed of death." He also speaks of the "womb" of death. Thinking of suicide, Antony clearly associates eroticism and death.

> I will be
> A bridegroom in my death, and run into't
> As to a lover's bed.

Cleopatra calls on death the way a woman might call on an impatiently expected lover: "Where art thou, death? / Come hither, come! Come, come, come, and take a queen." The erotic tone could not be more suggestive. In her mind, death assumes the shape of a skillful love partner: "The stroke of death is as a lover's pinch / Which hurts, and is desir'd"—a comparison that echoes Cleopatra's earlier reference to her suntanned complexion "with Phoebus' amorous pinches black." Love and death are further associated with sleep. About to apply the asp to her breast, Cleopatra sees herself as holding a baby "that sucks the nurse asleep."

Death is ultimately viewed as an aesthetic experience, a physical and metaphysical manifestation of beauty. Radiant deaths are not uncommon in Shakespeare's works, I reminded my students with a renewed touch of pedantry. Death is very often a moment of illumination and sublime accord.

"The tongues of dying men / Enforce attention like deep harmony," says a character in *Richard II*. It is hard to forget the musical deaths of Desdemona and Emilia, who both die singing the sad willow song. "I will play the swan / And die in music," says Emilia. Othello's own death signals a moment of peace and beauty, as he falls on Desdemona's bed, joining her in what he, too, experiences as love in death. "I kissed thee ere I killed thee: no way but this / Killing myself, to die upon a kiss." Even Gloucester, in *King Lear*, dies with a sense of joy: his heart "burst smilingly."

Death can seem a moment of transcendent beauty, but such beauty is not one of physical forms. It is not the kind of surface beauty that Octavius Caesar admires in front of inanimate Cleopatra:

> She looks like sleep
> As she would catch another Antony
> In her strong toil of grace.

The real beauty is perceived as a sense of peace coming with the supreme moment. Cleopatra's final words invoke this inner peace: "As sweet as calm, as soft as air, as gentle." A sense of beauty and peace that is clearly associated with the already mentioned motif of sleep. Antony's words at the end of act 4, as he decides to take his life, makes the point explicitly: "Unarm, Eros; the long day's task is done, / And we must sleep."

•   •   •

Death is cheated by the artifice that goes into the art of dying. Cleopatra's planned and staged *ars moriendi*—itself a form of deceit—leads to a self-willed statuesque pose and marblelike immobility that fulfill a new yearning for permanence and immortality. Cleopatra's words toward the end of the play make the point unambiguously: "I have /

immortal longings in me"; "I am fire and air; my other elements / I give to baser life."

In Shakespeare's account, Cleopatra's death is not merely another historical event; it conveys the essential meaning of the play. There is, to be sure, a substantial unity between Cleopatra's life and her death. She dies as she has lived, theatrically. It is not a "Roman" death. It is altogether voluptuous, imaginative, poetic. As Octavius Caesar reminds us in the closing lines, "She hath pursu'd conclusions infinite / Of easy ways to die." In more ways than one, it is an artistic death. But her ultimate artistry also signifies victory over herself—the final metamorphosis of the passionate and fickle human being. Cleopatra's new longing for permanence and constancy pervades all of act 5, culminating in the image of the statue.

Her other victory is over the apparently triumphant Octavius Caesar, whom she cheats out of a colorful, triumphal procession in Rome with her as captive. She even pities him because now, though all-powerful, he is more than ever Fortune's knave—and Fortune is a whore. She repudiates her own former frailties. She accuses her treasurer of being as untrustworthy as love that is hired. At every point, her words betray a new preoccupation with fidelity and permanence:

> I have nothing
> Of woman in me: now from head to foot
> I am marble constant

Marble constant—a striking image that blends the themes of art and statuesque permanence. Cleopatra hopes to outlive herself, as the monument outlives the city. Even the moon, associated with Isis and change, is now repudiated: "now the fleeting moon / No planet is of mine." Cleopatra becomes even more explicit as she is about to set out for that other Cydnus, and feels that she has "immortal longings."

From "riggish" to "marble constant": her earthly journey is completed. She sits on her marble throne, and Octavius Caesar, in spite of his pompous last words, never looked paler. Pale and perhaps perplexed, for how could the future emperor Augustus—the man who was to banish the poet Ovid—understand a metamorphosis in which love leads to death, and death to love, a metamorphosis in which change leads to permanence, and betrayal to superior fidelity?

5 · "Brombingo!"— Learning from Students

A loud yell coming from the balcony interrupted my lecture as I was glossing the sea images of a Hebrides vacation setting in Virginia Woolf's *To the Lighthouse*. It came from a student who had suddenly stood up in the front row of the balcony, crying out twice, full voice, what clearly sounded like "Brombingo!"—and then immediately sat down. Recalling incidents of political protests during the years of the Vietnam War, I first thought it was a battle cry, a call for student rebellion, a signal for a demonstration—at the very least a vociferous disapproval of what I was saying. Somewhat taken aback, I nonetheless went on with my lecture.

It turned out that the yell "Brombingo!" was the agreed-upon victory cry in an unusual bingo game promoted by the student magazine, *The Princeton Tiger*. A full page of that publication invited the students in my course to participate in a contest:

> Calling on all LIT141 students! Bring this game card to class, and when you've five spaces in a row, marvel at its phallic qualities, then stand up and yell . . . BROMBINGO!!!!!

After the five exclamation marks, there followed rows of boxes listing a number of expressions I seemingly favored, such as "narrative flow," "prolepsis," "temporal scheme," "diachronic structures," and "indirect discourse." My critical jargon. Also words and names that I liked to quote—most of them related to Thomas Mann's *Death in Venice*: "Pan," "epiphany," "Phaeax," "phallic," "Dionysius," "epicurean," "homoerotic"—names and expressions that apparently titillated the students. The first one able to check off five of these terms as they come up in a single lecture of mine was the winner.

When I was told what the yell "Brombingo!" was about, I felt rather touched, even flattered, by the implicit mocking. My lectures had entered student mythology! I took in a spirit of fun what struck me as affectionate teasing. For teasing is usually a sure sign of fondness. And playfulness, the ludic element, I told myself, should be at the heart of learning and of teaching. Playing with ideas is never a frivolous activity. This is when we are at our best. *Homo ludens*, indeed: the very nature of intelligence is to be ludic, or playful. And perhaps there is no more precious classroom lesson to impart, both by student and by teacher, than how to remain mentally agile, how to experiment with notions and concepts, no matter how questionable or outlandish they may seem.

My pleasure in facing students extended to various formats: the regular class, where dialogue and discussion are encouraged; more intimate seminars, where student presentations are required; lecture courses calling for a measure of theatricality, but also providing the sense of a collective experience. Eye contact was for me all-important. When I agreed to participate in a television lecture series, I felt dismayed by the absence of faces in front of me. The idea of talking to the lens of a camera was so inhibiting to me that I expressed my need for a visible audience in the recording room (even if they were street people, I jokingly added). The organizers of the program obliged, though I still wonder how and where they recruited the group.

Over the years, I have relished the singular elation in the classroom when the current between teacher and students passes, when students and teacher alike experience a time outside of time, when contact and exchange become part of a performance in which the entire group participates, when ideas become protagonists, and one is happy to teach and learn, often from one's students. The personal and collective affects of a literary work have always intrigued me. To what extent can one hope for a communality of responses? Reading is a private matter. Yet in teaching literature, one presumably seeks a common ground, and aims at translating subjective reactions into a coherent interpretation capable of accommodating individual responses. That special current in the classroom becomes a form of communion.

When I reflect on my nostalgia for decades of teaching, Wordsworth's striking image of "pensive citadels" often comes to mind. Harkness

Tower in New Haven and the bell tower of Nassau Hall in Princeton were indeed for me emblems of serene contentment in academic strongholds, especially after the chaos of World War II. To be sure, this nostalgia of mine is for an especially privileged era in privileged institutions—an era that recent generations might find hard to imagine, now that the humanities are threatened everywhere and traditional canons are discredited.

For many years I was, so to speak, on automatic pilot between home and campus. I hardly knew the names of the streets I took to reach my destination. In the early days, my infatuation with my chosen career led me at times to make extravagant statements. At a party where potent martinis were served, I scandalized a senior colleague, our host, by declaring (I had probably imbibed one martini too many) that our profession was so rewarding that one would gladly pay for the privilege of teaching. The colleague's grimace was eloquent. It taught me to moderate my enthusiasm.

Teaching did not come without a range of troubling thoughts and images magnified grotesquely in some bad dreams. In one recurrent nightmare, I am late, and arrive out of breath at the classroom building just as my students already rush down the staircase. I try to bar their way, to push them up the stairs back to our classroom. All in vain. I plead with them, but they pay no attention. They push to the wide-open front door and disappear. I remain standing in the hall, abandoned and disconsolate.

In another recurrent nightmare, I am lecturing in an immensely large auditorium. The students either look out the pseudo-Gothic windows or sit astride their chairs with their backs turned to me. Nobody pays attention to me or to what I am saying. And my voice gets increasingly feeble, becoming almost inaudible. In small groups, the students begin to leave the hall. Pleading with them to stay—I have important things to tell them—is of no use. They cannot even hear me. Soon the lecture hall is empty. Once again, I am left alone.

Even in those early teaching days, long before I was teasingly interrupted by a friendly game of Brombingo!, I saw my recurrent bad dreams as signs of a need for contact with my students.

•   •   •

My much-admired mentor, Henri Peyre, taught by example that the function of a teacher in the humanities was not to inculcate and expect

intellectual obedience from submissive disciples but to stimulate, to provoke, to juggle concepts, to help students discover their own thoughts
and develop their own voices. (My wise and skeptical father, much
earlier—I was still a child—had urged me to hold all self-proclaimed
authority in suspicion, reminding me to beware of all "dogma" and to
remember that much that is nasty stems from submission to doctrinaire teachings.) When I myself became a voice from the podium, I also
learned that I would be well advised to exercise some skepticism even
about myself, and that one could learn with and from one's students.

That lesson was brought home in my early teaching days at Yale when
I was recruited, together with a few other young instructors, to participate in a special program for a hundred or so selected freshmen enrolled
for intensive, coordinated studies in literature, philosophy, and art history. The ten young instructors in the literature component were each in
charge of a discussion section and took turns giving the two weekly lectures to the entire group—though normally not on a subject within their
own field of specialization. We all learned a lot in the program. Having
to read and discuss works with which we were not really familiar meant
being just a little ahead of our students. It was the best training. We also
learned how to organize a course, how to plan a syllabus. The readings in
this Directed Studies program seemed to follow a rational plan. The fall
term was devoted to the tragic tradition, going back to the book of Job in
the Bible, moving to Aeschylus and Sophocles, and then to Shakespeare
and some modern writers. The spring term dealt with the epic tradition,
and some of its echoes in more recent works. We began with Homer's
Odyssey, proceeded to Virgil's *Aeneid* and Milton's *Paradise Lost*, and
wound up the year's course with Alexander Pope's *Rape of the Lock* and
T. S. Eliot's *Waste Land*. The reading list had been designed by a senior colleague of the English department, who also directed the program.

What struck me after a while was that both fall and spring terms
related the end to the beginning. Our selected freshmen were guided
from the Bible to T. S. Eliot's notion of sin, and back again. My father's
admonitions were perhaps still echoing in my mind. I began to have
some misgivings. The not-so-hidden moral agenda at the heart of our
course prevented it, in my opinion, from being truly challenging. The
texts we read were all canonical and orthodox, altogether concerned
with sin, transgression, and human failings in the face of eternal values. No subversive or destabilizing work was included, no great novel,

no lyric poetry. The Bible and *Paradise Lost* set the tone. The historical background was hardly mentioned. Whiffs of eternity pervaded the lectures and the discussions. The students were at no point led to suspect that works of literature not grounded in accepted moral beliefs can be great and especially interesting—interesting because unconventional or deviationist perspectives are also part of the best human heritage.

It seemed to me that we might all learn together, and with profit, by reading an essay or two of Montaigne, whose restless, paradoxical mind excelled at questioning, even undermining, his own assumptions.

•   •   •

Not every colleague, I was aware, shared the belief that a scholar may be in intellectual need of students, that a professor could indeed learn with them, and from them. Looking down on students is a fairly common attitude among European academics, as I observed on numerous occasions while lecturing in France and Italy, where a professor expects to be treated with respect (and some diffidence) as authority incarnate. But even some American colleagues, used as they were to closer, even cordial relations with students, seemed to have some doubts about the intellectual benefits they themselves derived. "Do you really mean that you have ever learned anything from a student?" I remember being asked with a snicker by a colleague during a committee meeting.

More than ever did I value my own relations with students after observing the attitudinal gap between university students and their teachers in Italy, where I myself was subjected to the students' obsequious and vaguely distrustful treatment as a visiting professor in Pisa. More than ever I tried to make myself available once back on the American campus: in my wood-paneled office where students chatted with me at length, relaxing on an ancient sofa; at the *table française*, where I was joined for lunch by a group of young francophiles; on the way to the Sterling Library, exchanging views on an author we were reading just then; in the classroom, often filled with laughter, where I felt suddenly enlightened by an undergraduate's candid question or remark that helped me see a passage in a text, or an idea, in a new perspective.

When I was not sitting with my French-speaking students, I often joined a group at a long table in the college dining hall. On an early occasion, I recall being asked gently by one of them why I had joined their group. "You look awfully mature," he added with a slightly wicked smile. Very soon, however, I felt welcome to participate in their table talk. They would speak about their weekends, their extracurricular activities, the latest sports results. They apologized for talking about such trivial matters. You must find this quite boring, they said. Trivial matters? I reassured them. On the contrary. The subject of sports, for instance, was a serious matter. It touches on philosophical questions. A philosophy major concurred, bringing up time and space. We discussed specifics. Take boxing: the three minutes of the round, the twenty-by-twenty-feet dimension of the ring. Or take soccer: the rectangular field of determined length and width, the two official periods of the game lasting forty-five minutes each. These were all man-made rules and laws that mimic natural laws governing our lives, but also declare our freedom from the laws of nature, and thus affirm our free will. As we talked, I was aware that some sports did not quite adhere to this neat scheme. No matter; we had much fun debating these questions.

Soon we had regular mini-seminars at the lunch table. Our exchanges were no longer limited to weekend activities and sports events. We discussed books they were reading, and we raised questions about what it means to read, and how to read. Did literary works merely provide a higher form of entertainment, or was the printed word the revelation of a dialogue we carry on with ourselves? Opinions diverged, as they did about whether books were meant to instruct or to provoke. We also broached more controversial subjects. The collective memory of slavery as experienced by contemporary African Americans came up on a number of occasions, as did the plight of America's native populations. I was impressed by the students' sensitivity to social issues. Anti-Semitism was also discussed in its various forms—bigoted, snobbish, economic, racist, brutal, and plain ignorant.

I was an undeniable beneficiary of these table talks, as I was of my students' reactions to the books we read and analyzed in my courses. My conviction that scholarship in the humanities stands to gain from teaching stems, at least in part, from the repeated experience of writing books about authors or themes first discussed in the classroom. My *Romantic Prison* began to take shape when, in totally unrelated courses, I taught Stendhal's *The Charterhouse of Parma*, Shakespeare's *King Lear* ("let's away to prison"), and Dostoevsky's *Notes from the House of the Dead*. Similarly, my book on Victor Hugo surely originated when, at the time of the Vietnam War, I put Hugo's short early novel *The Last Day of a Condemned Man* on our reading list. To my astonishment and delight, that book became the students' favorite reading that term. They were struck by the modernity of the first-person narrative and admired young Hugo's fearlessness in writing this fervent indictment of capital punishment. They were impressed by the terseness of the language, relished the black humor, were moved by the clinical account of fear and appalled by the obscene curiosity of the populace rushing to witness the spectacle of a beheading. Above all, they almost unanimously endorsed Hugo's central thesis that capital punishment was a cold-blooded murder committed by society in the name of the law. Our discussions, at the time our students were in a politically rebellious mood, greatly encouraged me to launch on a full-length study of Hugo's defiant novels.

•   •   •

A touch of narcissism, I must admit, insinuates itself into the satisfactions of the podium. What lecturer has not dwelt complacently on the audience's appreciative reactions and the echo of the applause? (What author has not lovingly fondled the recently published book?) But there also come moments of doubt, even a sense of failure. There is, however, a lesson to be learned from such moments of utter frustration—and that lesson may also come from one's students.

More than once, when encountering former participants in my classes, I was astonished by the discrepancy between their recollections and my own. I was in the habit of grading myself. Sometimes severely. There was that day when I left the classroom with a nagging sense of inadequacy. I had tried to define existentialism. During much of the hour, I had been searching for the correct terms, coming up with mere approximations, muddling issues. Several times, trapped in a series of non sequiturs, I lost my train of thought. Yet several years later, when I was greeted by a former student at an airport, she declared that, yes, she had liked my course, but that there was one lecture of mine that she had found especially engrossing and could not forget. It happened to be the very one during which I had felt so uncomfortable, which had made me feel so inadequate, so incoherent.

I was taken aback. But I also began to understand—it was a precious lesson—that what my student had retained as so positive was precisely what had distressed me: my struggle with words, my struggle with ideas and concepts. It was a struggle that also engaged the students. Conversely, I now suspect that on days I was pleased with myself and thought that my lecture had gone especially well, the class may have judged me glib, perhaps even pompous. It was perhaps on one such occasion that I was interrupted by the loud cry of "Brombingo!"

Lessons learned from students could be even more effective in a seminar setting. While still a fledgling instructor, I was entrusted with a graduate seminar on the very subject of my doctoral dissertation. Like many another fresh PhD., I wanted to pour out all the knowledge I had accumulated and display my command over a wide range of complexities. I spoke far too much, and I spoke too fast. I wanted to go without delay to subtle abstractions, to theoretical questions concerning rhetoric and narrative structure, to the interplay of memory and imagination in the author's work. My students, as I was made to realize, would rather have discussed the social issues involved, the psychology and motivation of the fictional characters, the Marxist or Freudian interpretations of the texts we studied.

I came to realize that my students had a point in offering resistance to my theoretical divagations. With time, I learned to avoid giving the impression that I was in possession of privileged insights into the secrets of an author's achievement, and that it was my mission to reveal them to others as though I was their appointed guardian.

The lesson—it prepared me for the humorous game of Brombingo!— went beyond my own case. Struck by the variety of my students' challenging comments and interpretations, I began to see more clearly that although reading remains essentially a private affair, the study of literature, at least in the classroom, is by its very nature a collective effort, a meeting of sensibilities, a concert of ideas.

Part II · The Ludic Mode

6 · The Paradox of Laughter

Why would Giacomo Leopardi, Italy's supreme poet of hopelessness and despair, consider writing a history of laughter? His poetic message of gloom could not be clearer. In a short poem of 1833, "To Himself" ("A se stesso"), he dismisses all illusions, insists on the bitterness of life, and deplores the "infinite vanity" of everything. "The Infinite" ("L'Infinito"), perhaps his most celebrated poem, concludes with a suicidal wish of drowning ("naufragar") in the ocean of immensity. So why the wish to write a history of laughter?

The answer may possibly come from Leopardi's enigmatic essay "In Praise of Birds" ("Elogio degli ucelli"), which exalts the lightweight, feathered, and winged species as the "happiest creatures" in a tragic world. Unlike the scientifically curious Leonardo da Vinci, Leopardi was not interested in the movement of the birds' wings and tails, or in how the motion of air affected their flight. Nor was he concerned about how humans might turn their thoughts to flying themselves.

What fascinated Leopardi in his essay on birds was that they seemed to be the only cheerful creatures in an otherwise grim and hopeless world. They sing, and the more contented they are, especially when amorous, the better they sing. More surprisingly, Leopardi identifies their song as laughter ("riso"). This is no doubt the paradoxical part of the essay. One normally assumes that laughter is a human faculty, a human privilege; but Leopardi defines the human being as an "animale risibile," a creature more laughable than laughing. According to the poet, humans have indeed no business laughing; they are the most tortured ("travagliata") and most miserable of species. If humanity resorts to laughter, it is unfailingly a bitter laughter provoked by the perception of the vanity of everything, the vanity of life itself. Human laughter is never truly joyful as is that of birds! Crying ("pianto") comes in fact first for human beings, as is clear from the moment of emergence from the womb. Leopardi claimed that he would like to be transformed into a bird, so as to enjoy their very special joyfulness. Implicit is the abstract notion that laughter had to be invented by humanity because life would otherwise prove to be intolerable. These thoughts, it would seem, lie behind Leopardi's unrealized wish to write a history of laughter.

·   ·   ·

The fundamental bitterness of human laughter is hardly an idea invented by Leopardi. The Bible—see Proverbs—could not be more explicit: "Even in laughter the heart is sorrowful; and the end of that mirth is heaviness." Poets in more recent times have elaborated on that note. In one of the cantos of *Don Juan*, Lord Byron gave it a pungent formulation:

> And if I laugh at any mortal thing,
> 'Tis that I may not weep.

These lines seem to echo Beaumarchais's Figaro: "I hasten to laugh about everything, for fear of having to cry."

Philosophers of all periods have puzzled over the nature of laughter, and its complicity with the darker, violent side of life. In *The Republic*, Plato stated the link between laughter and violence: "When any man indulges in excessive laughter, it is almost always followed by an equally violent reaction." The passage comes in a discussion of the loud laughter of the Olympian gods when Hephaestus, god of blacksmiths, shows them his naked, adulterous consort Aphrodite with her lover, the god of war Ares, trapped in the invisible chain net he fabricated. It is obviously a mocking laughter. More recent philosophers developed this subject. In *Leviathan*, Thomas Hobbes famously maintained that laughter is an aggressive outburst, a "sudden glory" that comes from feeling superior to someone's inferiority.

Perhaps Friedrich Nietzsche has most bitingly characterized laughter as a tragic response to the terror of life. Certain memorable statements, notably in *The Will to Power*, confirm this somber view: "Man alone suffers so excruciatingly in the world that he was compelled to invent laughter." But laughter, according to Nietzsche, is also evil, as evidenced by Schadenfreude, wishing ill on others and rejoicing in their misery. Nietzsche thought that in laughter all that is evil comes together, that laughter can even kill.

·   ·   ·

But is laughter really that aggressive? Hobbes attributes it to a sense of "triumph" over the Other, to the joy of feeling superior. Nietzsche, always provocative, sees it as potentially lethal. The term "laughingstock" has passed into common usage—an expression that is hardly innocent of derogatory meaning, "stock" being the equivalent of butt or target, reminiscent of humiliating, torturous instruments, such as the whipping stock, or the wooden device for locking the feet and the hands of offenders at public punishments.

And there is something obtrusive, insistently physical, about the audible spasm of the respiratory system that goes under the name of laughter. Normally associated with loud sound, it has often been perceived as vulgar, aggressive, brutal, or nonsensical. The poet who denounced the loud laugh that speaks "the vacant mind" was only echoing Ecclesiastes' mordant comments about "the laughter of the fool." The disturbing mixture of silliness and potential violence in laughter transpires in many a popular expression. The French refer to *rire fou*—crazy, mad laughter. The Roman poet Catullus wrote peremptorily that there is nothing sillier than a "silly laugh." But worse than silly, the guffaw can also betray a grim view of circumstances, a distinctly perverse attraction to the darker side of life. In a letter to one of his friends, Charles Lamb (even though he knew a great deal about personal tragedy) confessed that "anything awful" made him laugh, that he had "misbehaved" at a funeral by breaking out in laughter.

The physicality of laughter is repeatedly brought home. One commonly hears of a belly laugh, of splitting one's sides, of laughing oneself into stitches. More than the vocal cords and the facial expression is involved. The reaction of laughter may be involuntary, like an automatic response of the body. "If you tickle us, do we not laugh?" Shylock's defensive words as an outcast Jew refer to a universal human reaction.

The wide range of laughter's causes and manifestations—peals or bursts of laughter, guffaws, snickers, Homeric roars—does not negate an underlying malevolence. A sneer of contempt is mild compared with the enormous injustice of the judgmental laughter recorded in the book of Job, where the just upright man, unjustly suffering from horrendous afflictions, is roundly mocked by his neighbors and "laughed to scorn." Mephistopheles, in various operatic versions of the Faust legend, is given to explosions of loud sarcastic laughter, to vocal displays of demonic derision. Satan does indeed laugh, and heartily, rejoicing with epic Schadenfreude as he goes about his business corrupting all innocence. One cannot imagine him smiling.

The smile is indeed totally alien to laughter. The smile is an elusive facial expression, never a material bodily sound. Unlike obtrusive laughter, the smile is private, silent, mysterious. It is perceived as gentle, tender, perhaps ever so slightly sad. Never hostile or disdainful. The most famous iconic smile, that of Leonardo da Vinci's *Mona Lisa*, has been stared at over the centuries by viewers trying to penetrate its secret. It has been described as more divine than human, as the outer manifestation of an ineffable inner self beyond our understanding.

Mephisto does not smile. And laughter remains totally foreign to the smile's benign and enigmatic nature. As for humor, irony, and satire, they only occasionally provoke laughter, and at that hardly a sonorous one. Humor, especially, is in a class apart, and to be savored quietly. Its nature is to be warm, protective, often defensive, making subdued fun of foibles—one's own or those of one's group. It can be a favored self-protection and self-recognition of the oppressed and persecuted. Humor can present "tribal" features: old family jokes passed on from generation to generation, a sense of solidarity and identity in the face of the hostile Other.

Irony is more devious. It requires swift decoding, as well as an interpretation. It does not aim to provide outbursts of hilarity; instead, it demands the instantaneous exercise and mobility of the intelligence. Irony is appreciated in silence. As for the censorious and corrective thrust of satire, traditionally serving in defense of threatened social norms, it excoriates excesses and vices endangering the stability of a supposedly wholesome social order, and performs its corrective functions without inciting boisterous exhilaration.

The limitations of all abstract (and arbitrary) discussions of laughter are perhaps best illustrated by the French philosopher Henri Bergson, whose treatise *Le rire* (*Laughter*) focuses on the social function of all comedy, excelling in the caricature of automatic human behavior: Molière's Miser acting as miser, his Misanthrope acting as misanthrope. This approach brings out the comic character's inability to adapt to reality (Don Quixote fighting the windmills; the distracted astronomer-scholar who keeps on walking, staring at the sky, and falls into a pit). The self-destructive failure to see things as they are, and where they are, is what, according to Bergson, makes us laugh. Bergson coined an oft-quoted formula for this automatic human behavior: "du mécanique plaqué sur du vivant" (something mechanical imposed on living matter). But this socially oriented, corrective laughter proves ultimately to be unkind, making fun of human beings who deserve our compassion. Bergson fails moreover to take into account a wide range of other causes and manifestations of hilarity, leaving out, at the very least, demonstrations of high spirits when laughter enters into unpredictably complicated relations, even into conflict, with changeable moods.

· · ·

The happy giggle of children comes to mind. But tears are never far off, as parents and attentive observers have always known. In an essay entitled "How We Cry and Laugh for the Same Thing," Montaigne uses children's rapid changes of mood as metaphors for the proximity of laughter to distress. Another kind of giggle, the giggle of embarrassment, coming from schoolchildren and certain childlike adults, though it can be endearing, is even less a manifestation of merriment. And what the French call a *rire jaune*—a sour laugh—is more closely related to displeasing, bitter thoughts than to euphoric sentiments.

Yet despite the opinion of respected philosophers that humanity is so miserable it was forced to invent laughter, and that this tragic laughter can also be aggressive, dismissive, self-righteous, mocking, contemptuous, sardonic, scornful, and even diabolical, there is sufficient evidence that laughter can also express positive feelings and attitudes: a sense of bonding, as when we laugh as a group at the theater; a sense of communion, for laughter can be contagious (although one sometimes fails to grasp what the others are laughing about); a sense of feeling nevertheless fully at home in what, at some discouraging moments, may seem like a senseless world. There is the laughter of simple, healthy satisfaction at being alive and active. And there is the strictly poetic laughter, the kind Lear dreams about as he envisages life with his daughter Cordelia in prison, where he expects that they will sing like birds in a cage and "laugh at gilded butterflies."

Laughter has also been associated with a measure of redemptive goodness. Thomas Carlyle thought that no person could be "irreclaimably bad" who had once wholly and heartily laughed. And Nietzsche, although he wrote that in laughter "all that is evil comes together" (that laughter, more than wrath, can kill), seemed to say almost the opposite when he maintained that we should consider every day without merriment as lost and call every truth a falsehood if it is not accompanied by at least one good laugh.

There is the expression "to fill one's heart with laughter." In a prayer-poem for children, Cardinal Spellman mentions "laughter's eager kiss." And lyric poets like to celebrate the seasons of love and laughter. But not for long. In some of their finest verses they sing of pain, darkness, and intimations of mortality.

• • •

Leopardi's beloved birds may well chirp so happily, and even laugh, because humanity is so miserable. According to the poet, humanity knows only the bitter laugh. But one is left to wonder whether, lurking beyond or behind his envious praise of the free-spirited *ucelli* there is not the conviction that sadness and empathy for suffering are morally superior to merriment. "Sorrow is better than laughter: for by the sadness of the countenance the heart is made better." This verse of Ecclesiastes was surely known to the erudite Italian poet. So must have been what follows: "The heart of the wise is in the house of mourning."

The Bible offers other affirmations of the moral superiority of sorrow and compassion. The already quoted words in Proverbs come to mind once again. "Even in laughter the heart is sorrowful."

7 · In Praise of Jealousy?

Why does God command the prophet Hosea to marry a whore? Hosea obeys and chooses as his wife a harlot named Gomer. The predictable happens: Gomer goes on whoring and abandons her husband. Yet when she wants to return to him, Hosea pardons her adulteries, turning his anger and his pain into forgiveness. It is a biblical lesson of supreme love.

But there is a deeper lesson in this story—a lesson God makes explicit. Hosea's bitter experience of betrayal is to be understood as the allegorical analog of the adulterous relations of the people of Israel who have fallen into adoring false gods. And just as Hosea was abandoned by his whorish wife, so God felt betrayed by the people of Israel guilty of idolatry.

In Exodus, and again in Deuteronomy and in Ezekiel, God is called the jealous God, ready to punish, but also to show mercy and to forgive (how can a father destroy his children?). He is a consuming fire to those unfaithful to him but full of divine love for those who return. The notion of divine jealousy is from the beginning inseparable from monotheism. God is unique. He is alone, not just because he is abandoned by Israel's idolatrous behavior, but because he is exclusively the Only One. The God of the Old Testament thus offers the masculine model of the legitimate and possessive husband, as well as the stern yet loving father figure.

During the same year that an undergraduate seminar made me vaguely familiar with divine jealousy in several biblical texts, I was by coincidence offered an altogether different insight into a strictly human jealous experience. Reading Marcel Proust in another course, I relived, at the beginning of his great novel, the narrator's boyhood apprenticeship of jealous suffering, when his mother, instead of coming to his bedside to kiss him once more, remains with her guests in the dining room—that forbidden space where his imagination situates the fiendish festivities, the "*fête inconcevable, infernale*" from which he is excluded. I understood from those opening pages that there is no jealousy without imagination, without the invention of a scene or scenario from which one is absent. Proust's narrative account of young Marcel's pain also suggests the link between the jealous projection of images and the literary imagination. The repeated references, later in the novel, to the little boy's jealousy caused by the unavailability of his mother, and the parallel the narrative voice establishes between that early initiation in childhood and the experiences of adult erotic jealousy, only confirm the overarching theme of literary creativity in Proust's work.

This was altogether different from divine jealousy. The jealous God does not need imagination. He is omniscient and omnipresent. He sees perfectly well the idolatrous behavior of the chosen people. He has a clear vision of the land that has committed "great whoredom." Human jealousy, on the other hand, never has clear vision, or any vision at all. It is inconceivable without imagination.

Othello is jealous because of the vivid images his mind projects as he remembers Desdemona's pleasure in his arms, which now, spurred by Iago's obscene remarks, obsesses him as he conjures up images of her even greater pleasure in the arms of a rival. Without the bite of a creative imagination, no real jealousy would seem possible. The obtuse Charles Bovary, on the other hand, does not succeed in feeling jealous. Even when he finds out the truth after Emma's death, the best he can do is to come up with the banal statement "It was the fault of fatality."

•   •   •

Jealousy has a bad reputation. It has traditionally been denounced as a shameful, reprehensible, demeaning passion. A ridiculous one, to boot. Anna Karenina's worldly brother Oblonsky, who likes to display his French, considers his sister's pathological suspicion of her lover Vronsky—and her retrospective jealousy of his former liaisons—"*du dernier ridicule*," utterly ridiculous. As for the cuckold, commonly portrayed with infamous horns on his forehead, he has for centuries been the subject of comedy and the butt of vulgar scorn. Shakespeare, in the springtime song of *Love's Labour's Lost*, gives this mockery a poetic form. But the masculine fear of contempt comes vividly across:

> The cuckoo then, on every tree
> Mocks married men; for thus sings he,
> Cuckoo,
> Cuckoo, cuckoo! O word of fear,
> Unpleasing to a married ear!

Othello is hardly a comic figure, but he is fully aware that a "horned man" is a laughable monster and, as he puts it, a beast. Even Shakespeare's great Roman leader Antony, in a moment of uncontrollable anger, believing that Cleopatra is a "triple-turn'd whore," imagines himself outroaring the "horned herd." The humiliating male fear of the cuckold's horns knows no national boundaries. Dostoevsky's "eternal husband" is shamefully convinced that he is carrying the disgraceful ornaments on his forehead; and Mister Ford, in Verdi's opera about Falstaff, bellows in a jealous outburst the Italian words for horns, *"Le corna, le corna!"*

Rational thought has traditionally dismissed fear of erotic betrayal, and jealousy in general, as unworthy of a reasonable human being. The French philosopher Montaigne, who lived in daily familiarity with Stoic and Epicurean thinkers of antiquity, denounced jealousy in one of his essays as "the most vain and tempestuous malady" afflicting a human soul. Otherwise open-minded and firmly opposed to prejudice, Montaigne believed that women especially are subject to this malady and cannot be cured of their inclination to be feverishly suspicious and jealous, behaving intolerably, with head-splitting screams and a desire for vengeance.

Misogynic reprobation of female erotic anger goes back to the ancient world, even to the Olympian seat of the Greek gods. Hera, the jealous and punishing wife of Zeus, famously torments him with her tantrums. (Jealous ire was the privilege of men.) The Roman view of women's jealousy is hardly more flattering. The poet Ovid, in his *Ars amatoria* (*The Art of Love*), speaks of women's anger when they are consumed by the flames of jealousy, becoming fierce as boars, madder than adders when stepped on, raving as frantic maenads. Ovid reminds his reader of the jealous rage of "barbarous" Medea who killed her children to punish their father, the unfaithful Jason.

With Medea's murder of her own children, an act of vengeful retribution, the evil effects of jealousy are raised to the noble level of high tragedy. Giulia Sissa has written eloquently about such awe-inspiring anger in her passionate and learned book, *Jealousy: A Forbidden Passion*. In spite of the prestige of a Medea or a Clytemnestra, further infuriated by Agamemnon's return from Troy with a concubine, such erotic anger is not the monopoly of women. Men, in different literary traditions, seem to have a special entitlement to jealous wrath. Giovanni Malatesta, in Dante's *Inferno*, murders his wife Francesca and his own brother Paolo, who is her lover—a case of extreme jealousy that binds the adulterous pair, tossed and blown through the air by a relentless wind for all eternity. Woyzeck, the eponymous hero of Georg Büchner's antiheroic tragedy, is driven mad by Marie's promiscuities and stabs her to death. Opera is especially rich in acts of jealous violence. Don José kills Carmen to the accompaniment of triumphal music glorifying his successful rival, the bullfighter. This murder scene below the walls of the arena reenacts a ritualistic or even demonic love-death celebration.

The most extreme indictment of jealousy stems from its association with the demonic. Iago calls this reviled passion a "green-eyed monster" capable of corroding all innocence. It is the work of a "*demon infernal*," according to King Philip, who ends up planning the death of his own son in Verdi's *Don Carlo*. Goethe, in his account of Werther's sufferings, refers to jealousy (*Eifersüchtig*) as a *Teufel*—a devil. And Tolstoy, in a still different linguistic context, calls Anna Karenina's suicidal crises of jealous passion the work of a *bes* (demon), the work of a *diavol*. Only magic, it would seem, can free one from such a curse. Which is what Puck, in *A Midsummer Night's Dream*, manages to achieve, but only thanks to the magic eyedrops provided by Oberon—and in a world of total fantasy.

•   •   •

The tarnished, if not downright infamous, reputation of jealousy throughout history—whether considered ludicrous, shameful, dangerously irrational, pathological, leading to acts of violence inspired by evil spirits—has little in common with the poetic pain experienced by young Marcel in Proust's novel, when his mother fails to come to his bedside to give him that appeasing goodnight kiss, entertaining instead her guest Monsieur Swann (the prestigious rival for the evening) and making the disconsolate boy feel abandoned and rejected as he imagines the scene of devilish festivities down on the floor below.

Proust has taught us, or rather confirmed, the lasting truth that no jealousy is conceivable without the work of the imagination, and conversely, by extension, that no work of the imagination is conceivable without some form of jealousy. To understand that apparent paradox, one needs to consider the nature of erotic jealousy.

The passion of jealousy—for it is a passion in every sense of that word—is not to be confused with ordinary envy. The two may occasionally overlap. But envy is never blind. It sees the object of its desire clearly. The jealous sufferer, on the other hand, is by definition sightless, or largely so. Blind to what is feared or suspected. The sufferer lives in a state of doubt, seeking an elusive truth, constructing scenarios that cannot be verified, no matter how intensive the detective work and how great the inquisitorial talents. Even a confession of the guilty partner cannot satisfy the quest for the full truth. The jealous being continues to be excluded from the acts and the scenes of betrayal—scenes that with time become ever more exquisitely painful, mysterious, and unreachable.

The gnawing pain of jealousy arises from one's demand for exclusive possession of the Other, and the fear or conviction that the Other is essentially free, and uses that freedom in order to escape. The fear of the Other's freedom implies a range of psychological complexities. The sense of loss of what is deemed a rightful possession comes close to a feeling of bereavement (how can this be taken away from me!), and is linked to intimations of total vulnerability. It can sap self-esteem, leading to what Stendhal defined as *imagination renversée*—inverted imagination—namely, seeing oneself as inferior. As for blindness in jealousy, it ironically leads to imagined voyeurism—imagining oneself peering into the sinful alcove. (Does not Iago suggest that Othello might wish to "behold her topp'd"?) Not to mention the process of revision over time, and the distorting operations of memory (new details and new clues come back) that display the changing faces of the suspected and unstable truth.

A quite different temporal dimension of jealousy may lead back in time, distressingly so, to the past love life of the lover, to earlier erotic experiences over which one cannot even hope to have any control. One can only imagine unfavorable comparisons. Anna Karenina increasingly suspects, with anger and self-hate, that Vronsky is still seeing an actress, a former mistress from the time he frequented theater people. The previous life of her lover excludes her entirely. Similarly, the adult Marcel in Proust's *In Search of Lost Time* suspects that Albertine, whom he would like to hold prisoner in his Paris apartment, still manages to meet lovers from before he knew her—lesbian lovers, what is more! The possessively surveilled Other, ever more evasive, becomes for him an unfathomable stranger in her unreadable past.

An even more deeply painful time-dimension of jealousy is future-oriented, pointing to hypothetical afterlife visions of the beloved initiating a new life with a posthumous rival. Such a devastating betrayal of expected fidelity in a future from which one is totally absent may for some be the ultimate image born of the fear of nonexistence.

·   ·   ·

The figure of the rival in the complex relation to both desire and jealousy has been brilliantly analyzed by René Girard in his *Deceit, Desire, and the Novel*. According to Girard, all forms of love, all forms of desire and jealousy, are subject to the laws of a triangular structure—a pattern that depends on the mental presence of a rival. It would follow, even if one may question some of Girard's rigid theoretical developments, that the mimetic character of desire implies a typical love/hate fascination, a secret admiration of the rival.

This intricate obsession with the rival is nowhere brought out more artfully than in Dostoevsky's *The Eternal Husband*. Trusotsky, the cuckolded husband who feels doomed to wear on his forehead the infamous horns, meets his wife's former lover long after the affair, and after his wife's death. Or rather, he seeks him out and, in scenes of tragic buffoonery filled with Dostoevskyan self-humiliation and self-abasement, reveals ambiguous feelings toward his wife's seducer. He is ready to cut his throat with a razor knife, yet he treats him lovingly. This not-so-secret affection and admiration for the hated rival corresponds to loss of self-esteem, even to a sense of emasculation.

Trusotsky's conflictual emotions about the successful rival are neither new nor exceptional. Goethe's Werther, in a totally different context of amorous jealousy, also dreams of violence (as well as friendship with "the best man in all creation"), and at the same time feels like a man "stripped of his sword"—a long-standing image for being unmanned.

The need for a rival in order to properly experience desire, the need for jealousy in order to love or rekindle love—those seem to be timeless needs summed up laconically by the Latin adage "*qui non zelat, non amat,*" whoever is not jealous does not love.

•   •   •

In a lighter vein, the Roman poet Ovid, offering all sorts of useful and colorful tips to would-be lovers in his *Art of Love*, specifically recommends jealousy as an erotic stimulant. This elegant didactic poem (Ovid signs off as *magister*—teacher) provides practical advice about a number of questions: where in Rome to meet pretty women (the neighborhood of a Syrian synagogue is one of the recommended places; so are the law courts, Pompey's column, the portico of the Danaïdes); how to approach a woman in a stadium (do not be shy, and in passing do brush her thigh); how to gain access to her by making promises, and how in turn to tolerate lies. In a special section of advice to women on how to keep passion alive, the *magister* (not failing to mention proper body hygiene) recommends above all the art of provoking jealousy as a stimulant and aphrodisiac. Ovid could not have known, but would have appreciated, the French saying that one is never so good at lovemaking as with an unfaithful woman. Whoever first formulated this somewhat scabrous observation was surely aware of the central role of the imagination in fueling jealousy, and of the galvanizing effect of the feared rival.

Stendhal's love lessons in *The Red and the Black*, and even more explicitly in his treatise *On Love*, make much the same point. They even go one step further, declaring the priority of jealousy over love. Julien Sorel's ultimate success in the siege of Mathilde de La Mole comes entirely as a result of having learned to provoke her intense jealousy. Even more specifically in his essay on love, amorous passion is defined as a "fever of the imagination"—a fever kept at high pitch by doubt and suspicion. Arguing in favor of the jealous imagination, Stendhal goes so far as to assert that all "happiness in love" depends on a degree of jealous insecurity. "Toujours un petit doute à calmer"—always some doubt, some distressing suspicion, in need of being assuaged. And in a poetic passage of this very personal essay, Stendhal refers to the "jardins en-chantés de l'imagination," the magical gardens of the imagination.

Pain-inducing jealousy and provocative jealousy can of course inter-act. The example of Tosca, in Puccini's opera, comes to mind, when the diva playfully and a trifle dramatically (she is after all truly suspicious at some point) makes use of her theatrical talents and erotically effective questions in the opening church scene with her lover Cavaradossi. Her partly genuine, partly enacted recriminations inflame her own erotic mood. It all leads to an appointment to spend the night together. The imagined infidelity of her lover, and its effect on her, confirms that jeal-ousy is not conceivable without the work of the imagination. Evil Scarpia knows this, when, like another Iago, he rekindles her erotic anger with hints and suggestions that feed that jealous imagination.

The poetic potential of jealousy has in fact been the subject of many an operatic aria. Baroque operas are especially rich in distressed protag-onists singing with lengthy embellishments about their grief in lyrical lamentations that nourish or revive their love. Handel's "Scherza infida" ("You jest, unfaithful one, in the arms of your lover") in *Ariodante* is ar-guably the most moving of all his arias. The baroque operatic repertoire is studded with words referring in great musical beauty to erotic treason: "*infedele*," "*tradita*," "*gelosia . . . tiranna*."

· · ·

It is hardly surprising that adultery and jealousy have been such privi-leged subjects in narrative art. Even a cursory glance at Denis de Rougemont's *Love in the Western World* informs the reader that, ever since the literature of the troubadours and of courtly love, poetry and fiction have insistently treated adultery, and concomitant jealousy, as passionate adventures of the human spirit. The word *passion*—from the Latin *pati* and *passio* (suffering, enduring)—is especially appropriate for the experience of jealousy. It may even be a welcome suffering, as Rougemont seems to imply. The ordeal may secretly be wished for and, as he provokingly suggests, one may come to desire that the loved one be unfaithful so as to revive desire and renew the pursuit.

It is linguistically revealing that the word "jealousy" is derived from the Greek *zëlos*, from which we also have the word "zeal," with its conno-tations of effort and ardent interest, of striving, seeking, and searching.

Interrogations, surveillance, and investigations are of the essence in the jealous quest for knowledge. We must return to Proust, for nowhere is this inquisitional effort illustrated more strikingly than in the pages devoted to Marcel's troubled affair with Albertine, whose every move he checks and counterchecks, even enlisting his chauffeur as chaperone and spy. Marcel's obsessive questions about Albertine's errands and appointments display more than a simple need to find out about her activities. It corresponds to a *"soif de savoir"*—an unquenchable thirst for knowledge. But the Other remains an unknowable secret, and the truth unreachable.

The essential blindness of the jealous sufferer, the thwarted need and hope to uncover the truth and obtain full view of the feared scene, leads unavoidably to imaginary voyeurism. This unseeing intrusion may take an indirect or oblique form, as when Marcel interrogates his chauffeur about Albertine's appointments or, more dramatically, when Golaud, in Maeterlinck's and Debussy's *Pelléas et Mélisande*, questions the little boy (his son), who has spent time in the company of the suspected love pair. Do they stand close to each other? What do they talk about when they are together? Do they quarrel? Do they kiss? When they meet, do they stand close to a bed? Golaud concludes that he will never know, that he is like an *aveugle*, a blind person who is seeking for a treasure at the bottom of an ocean.

It is not by chance that the French word *jalousie* (as well as the Italian *gelosia*) also denote a latticed window *blind* made of wood or metal, through which one can see without being seen. This special use of the word may correspond to the hope—a vain hope of course—that jealousy is not really blind and can witness the betrayal. The ironic Swiss novelist Max Frisch has played with this idea in *Gantenbein*, whose protagonist pretends to be really and totally blind so as to be able to surveil the activities of his unfaithful wife. He has managed to procure all the accoutrements of a certified blind person (the cane, the yellow armband, the blind man's glasses) and is able to watch his wife appear at the airport, brazenly accompanied by her lover who carries her coat—thus becoming the secret spectator of scenes he would normally not see, but only imagine. By a fictional twist of the usual situation, it is the jealous husband who is more secretive than his adulterous (and unsuspecting) wife. He possesses her secret; she does not possess his. But this, once again, is in a world of fantasy.

The very real and distressing blindness that goes with jealousy is of course the deeper truth below Max Frisch's ironic inventiveness, and constitutes the subject of much fiction-making. Anna Karenina, an avid reader of English novels (she never travels without reading one in her train compartment), constructs novels in her own mind about devastating adulterous betrayals as she watches people waiting at the railroad station just before she commits suicide. Tolstoy evidently understood the fiction-inventing urge of the jealous mind.

This fiction-making propensity, at least in a literary perspective, could be singled out as the exceptional positive feature of jealousy. But is it really so exceptional? Without listing the erotically stimulating virtues of jealousy and its potential for vivifying love (ideas dear to Ovid and Stendhal), and without invoking accounts of forgiveness and ensuing greater fidelity, a case can been made for the instructive nature of emotional pain. Proust, to whom we return as to a more modern magister, insists at great length in *The Captive* and in *Time Regained* on the revelatory nature of amorous grief. Jealousy may be a "chronic malady" nurtured by the imagination ("My jealousy was born of images"), but the ultimate stress is on the fecundity of sorrow. "Happiness is good for the body, but it is sorrow that develops spiritual strength" ("la force de l'esprit"). Or again, striking remarks about the searing but precious heartbreak ("déchirement précieux") that makes the misery of amorous treason and loss eventually so fruitful.

Fruitful in what way? Proust gives a surprising answer. Fruitful because of the "truths" that the lover's betrayal helps us discover. The "truths" in question obviously go beyond the guilty activities of the unfaithful one. The jealous mind may originally be searching for distressing evidence and full knowledge of the betrayal. But the "truths" discovered correspond to a deeper quest reflected in the tortuous sentences and sinuous syntax of Proust's prose, filled with subordinate clauses, indirections, and digressions. This arduous and much broader quest linked to the notion of jealousy is defined as one of the great "*plaisirs de l'intelligence*"—an elation of the intellect facing the mysteries of life. The ultimate truth, however, remains unknowable.

In declaring the fertility of the jealous imagination, Proust clearly has in mind its value to himself, the creator of fiction, in dealing with the world of possibilities. There may be no jealousy without imagination, but perhaps the obverse also is true. Imagination is not without some form of jealousy. This proposition of an inverted relationship between imagination and jealousy may, on the face of it, seem strange, but it is convincingly illustrated in a remarkable experimental novel by Alain Robbe-Grillet, *La jalousie*, which treats the all-absorbing experience of jealousy as both object and subject. The writing itself, as well as the reading, become exercises in jealous surveillance. The French title of the novel, which unfolds in a colonial setting, refers to the jealous passion, but also to a physical object *(une jalousie)*—the blind allowing the unnamed jealous protagonist (who is also the narrator and the narrative voice) to watch a regularly visiting neighbor sip aperitifs on the terrace with his suspected wife, identified only as A. The observing husband-narrator remains invisible and mute. The entire novel is constructed around watching and listening. But the nameless husband-observer does not really "see," and he cannot interpret correctly what he hears or overhears. There is no chronological or sequential development. Jealousy is obsessively repetitive. The past and the immediate future are in the present. Events and their perception occur in a permanent *now*. Everything is registered, nothing is erased. Words and gestures have multiple meanings. Imagination is feverishly at work, exacerbated by the heat on the colonial plantation, as distant wild animal cries take on ominous erotic significance in the mind of the suspicious observer. Partial or impaired vision, ambivalent overheard syllables, hummed tunes to which the wife and the plantation neighbor may or may not have danced together—all these undecidable indices compel the reader as well to experience the events narrated in a state of doubt, anxiety, and suspicion.

•   •   •

Robbe-Grillet's literary achievement in *La jalousie*—an undeniable tour de force—extends and illustrates Proust's implicit praise of the jealous imagination. But even an admiring reader and lover of literature may wonder whether Robbe-Grillet has captured how in real and more prosaic life most people experience the pangs of jealousy. Imagination is surely always at work, and can be hauntingly creative. But do the scenes and scenarios it conjures up so vividly and painfully, do the truths about the self and the human condition that the *soif de savoir* discovers, compensate for the misery that comes with betrayal in love? Positive aspects of the jealous passion can be invoked: the search for knowledge, a deeper understanding of oneself, the revelation of forgiveness and greater love. And there are some more lighthearted views of jealousy's erotic virtues (notions dear to Ovid and Stendhal), and also of the dreamlike ability to dispel its evil effects through midsummer nights' magic. More commonly, however, jealousy doubtless remains for most a bitter ordeal, generating not creative energy, precious insights, and renewal of love, but anguish, anger, and the wish for avenging retribution.

This apparent disparity between intense suffering and the creative work of the mind raises the broader question of the unceasing shuttle and interaction between works of the imagination (the books we read, the images we see) and the raw lived experience, between art and life, between the mediated and the unmediated experience.

8 · On Rereading

In my pandemic confinement, staring at the bookcases in my study, packed with so many great books that have remained unread, I hear my own nagging voice—"Shame on you!" It's now or never. Blaise Pascal's words about contentment in the solitude of one's room echo in my mind. I should feel grateful, I say to myself, and take full advantage of my claustration, now that I spend more time than ever at my desk, surrounded by the books amassed over the years. There is no longer any excuse for leaving these masterpieces unread.

The first volume I picked up was Giovanni Boccaccio's *Decameron* in the original Italian, perhaps because I vaguely remembered that the book's licentious stories are told against the background of a collective calamity. In my early teens, I had found some erotic titillation in surreptitious glances at passages in the modern translation belonging to my mother. I had no idea at the time that the seven young women and the three young men who tell each other these salacious stories had escaped from the Black Death and found refuge in a villa located in the hills overlooking their afflicted city. And so, a lifetime later, I resolved to read Boccaccio at last.

Surprise! Boccaccio's "Introduzione" (which I had never bothered to look at in my mother's copy) was not in the least frivolous or erotic, but gave a detailed, graphic account of the deadly pestilence, the "mortifera pestilenza," that devastated Florence in 1348. The symptoms of the virulent epidemic disease are described very precisely: blood flowing from the nose, buboes ("gavòccioli") the size of an egg or even an apple in the groin or under the armpits, large black spots on arms and thighs as well as other parts of the body. The reader is not spared references to the stench of corpses all over the city. Deplorable human reactions are reported: citizens feeling disgust for one another, brother abandoning brother, wife abandoning husband. Even children are abandoned. People think of saving only themselves—and, if they can afford it, fleeing from the city. All this was new to me.

But I was in for another surprise. On the second page of Boccaccio's stark account of the Florentine pestilence, I discovered in the margins (I could hardly believe my eyes) what clearly was my own somewhat faded handwriting, as well as various sentences or expressions I had underlined. So I had read the "Introduzione" after all—and in the original Italian! But what I was rereading seemed entirely new.

This puzzled me. It also encouraged me to pick up another classic I had postponed reading for years: my long-neglected bilingual edition of Ovid's *Metamorphoses*, the Roman poet's collection of epic narratives about mythological figures and their eventual transfigurations. The name of Ovid had occasionally been on my lips in the classroom, but I could not honestly say that I was familiar with his poem. And so I opened my volume, turning first to the pages devoted to the ill-fated love of Pyramus and Thisbe (a mythological Romeo and Juliet couple), reduced by parental disapproval to whisper their love for each other through a crack in the wall. Then I moved to the well-known story of Orpheus rescuing his Eurydice from the underworld, only to lose her again. And again, to my surprise, I found my handwritten remarks in the margins, and entire sentences underlined. Only this time, I wondered: Why did I underline this sentence or line? It's the next one that is important!

Clearly, my way of reading the text had shifted, and I myself had changed over the years.

.   .   .

This raised the larger question of rereading. It comes in many forms. There's voluntary rereading, the result of a willful decision to revisit a book one has admired, or a book that has left one with some unanswered questions. This kind of planned revisitation could also be for verifying certain details in the text, or for checking on the moves of a given character. A conscientious academic might also wish to refresh intimacy with a work, and thus avoid relying on the same old notes, or mumbling through the same fifteen-year-old written lecture with assured soporific effects.

Contrarily, there's what I had experienced with Boccaccio and Ovid, which could be defined as involuntary rereading. The original reading was either forgotten or so totally assimilated that the new chance encounter with the text produced surprise and astonishment. My reaction to the renewed reading no longer corresponded to the original experience, and I was no longer sure that I recognized myself as the same reader.

Then there are what one might call subconscious rereadings, those that occur without the specific act of reading, much as the memory of a tune can haunt the mind without actually being heard again. This form of remembered contact with a book can accompany us during a lifetime, and continue to nurture and shape us. Much in the same manner, we may over the years recite to ourselves poems learned by heart long ago, which have become part of our self-recognition.

And, finally, there is the rarer, quite precious experience that might be called "pre-reading," when certain dispositions in our character, coupled with circumstances, make us receptive in advance to an author we have not yet encountered. That is in substance what happened when, as a schoolboy, I occasionally skipped my science classes at the Parisian *lycée*, taking myself by métro to unfamiliar quarters of the capital in order to blend, incognito, with the crowds. The truant adolescent did not yet know the poetic use of the word *flâneur*, but those city walks prepared him to discover Baudelaire as though he had read him attentively before.

•   •   •

All of these ways of reading are valuable. But an actual rereading can lead to a more complex, more literary, understanding of a text, when the stress is no longer on the what but on the how—namely, the craft of the composition and the quality of the language. And there are surprises. Renewed contact with a novel or a poem can activate the autobiographical curiosity, the search for a better knowledge of the self. The new reading, a form of revision, uncovers the change in us. The newness is not in the text. It is we who have evolved. Every rereading registers this revision, and further provokes it. As the literary critic Rachel Falconer pertinently observed in introducing a collection of essays entitled *Re-reading/*

La relecture (2012), renewed encounters with a literary work make us feel, on every separate occasion, that we are reading it for the first time.

Books can transform us. They can determine a mental landscape, remake our vision of things, in much the way the advent of impressionism made people see both cityscape and landscape afresh. When Gustave Caillebotte painted a Paris street in the rain, or the teeming boulevard observed from his balcony, he opened his viewers' eyes to forms of beauty they did not suspect. Similarly, transformative readings—experiences after which one is no longer quite the same and one's outlook and sensitivity have been significantly altered—could be compared to a psychic rebirth involving the revelation of something new or, perhaps, the discovery of what was there already but as yet unrecognized.

Some of the greatest writers have always understood this, and they have made that shaping, transformative power of books the subject of their fictional work. Cervantes's demented Don Quixote, an obsessive reader of tales of chivalry, is driven by a compulsion to imitate the legendary knights-errant such as Amadis de Gaul. The effect of those chivalric romances on his mind alarms his familiars to the point of asking the priest and the barber to burn his books and then seal his library so he cannot find his way back to it.

Emma Bovary's romantic yearnings are similarly inflamed by books—namely, by novels and chronicles about passionate women and their great lovers, stories of steamy adulteries. She too burns to imitate her models, and live her own sexual adventures fully and dangerously. A lifelong admirer of Cervantes, Gustave Flaubert surely had *Don Quixote* in mind when Emma's mother-in-law proposes barring her from access to the noxious novels, offering to travel to Rouen in order to cancel Emma's subscription to the lending library, and if necessary to alert the police if the librarian persists in his poisonous trade.

As for Anna Karenina, she too is an inveterate reader of tales of love, while intent on living her own passionate affair to fictional extremes.

·   ·   ·

Most readers can surely distinguish between books admired, books from which one has learned, books that have unsettled and disturbed, and others—fewer no doubt—which have changed one forever. These distinctions are in all cases very personal. Names come to mind. Some figures from antiquity: Homer, Sophocles, Virgil. Certain masters of the novel: Balzac, Dostoevsky, Dickens. A few modernist writers: James Joyce, T. S. Eliot, Vladimir Nabokov, Virginia Woolf. All great, their works often moving and revelatory. But have they changed one's life? Have they altered one's vision of the world? Not in my case.

My childhood readings, on the other hand, even of a bizarre and unsettling nature, did enter my bloodstream. Many youngsters, especially in Europe, have been exposed to selected, often illustrated, passages of memorable episodes, such as the demented knight's attack on windmills he takes for hostile giants, or the humiliating events in the country inn where Sancho Panza is tossed in the air in a blanket by malevolent fun-seeking guests. For me, as a preadolescent, Don Quixote and Sancho Panza—the overheated idealizing brain and the realistic belly—became, in an as yet unformulated fashion, the complementary emblems of the spirit and the flesh. I vaguely understood that salvation, or rather sanity, lay in the sound balance between the two. Perhaps this understanding was a real beginning, after which I was no longer the same.

* * *

And after childhood? Whenever I ask myself which writers have determined my view of things, what literary works have helped shape my character, I come up, unsurprisingly in view of my *lycée* education, with the same three French authors: Proust, Stendhal, Montaigne—all three reread over the years, all three with a unique voice, but sharing some deep-seated common features.

The encounter with Marcel Proust goes back to my late teens, when a bookish older cousin of mine urged me to read *Swann's Way*. I realized very soon that something in me had been profoundly remade by these early parts of this very long novel. The pages about young Marcel's life with his family in Combray, and the vicissitudes of Swann's tormented love affair with Odette, changed my mental landscape. The narrator's boyhood experience of jealousy and of the jealous imagination became for me an apprenticeship in suffering, as I read, transfixed, about his mother who, instead of appearing as usual at his bedside to give him that ritualistic goodnight kiss, fails to show up, remaining instead with her guest—the child's rival that night—in the dining room downstairs, the site of a feverishly imagined festivity in which he cannot participate.

Instability and flux at the heart of Proust's narrative revealed to me that the frustrations and torments of love were ultimately beneficial to the creative spirit, and that, in view of the transience of everything, mental suffering, especially the unavoidable agony of love, was a "mal saeré" (sacred affliction) at the root of all art, our only chance of victory over evanescence and death.

Mobility and flux are surely also at the heart of Stendhal's work, though mostly in historical and social terms, and as manifestations of the author's intellectual agility. I discovered *The Red and Black* and *The Charterhouse of Parma*, as well as Stendhal's autobiographical writings, in my college years. His singular inner music, a blend of tenderness and irony (but an irony that protects the tenderness), altered the perception of my own identity. I began to see myself, or wished to see myself, as a lucid dreamer delighted to be taken in by my own dreams, a skeptical enthusiast watching himself live as though on a private stage. Stendhal became for me the model of mental freedom, and of the ability to reinvent oneself.

But the supreme lesson in flux came with my reading of the *Essays* by Michel de Montaigne, who has accompanied me ever since an admired mentor made me appreciate his restless curiosity, open-minded skepticism, and fondness for paradoxical ideas. Montaigne looked with equanimity at the other side of any argument. The protean nature of his thinking delighted me, as did the unpredictable twists and turns of his conversational style. I found wisdom in his readiness to cohabit with what the flesh is heir to. After absorbing hefty doses of his writings, my glance turned inward. I was impressed by his justification for the unremitting interest he took in himself. Others look outward, he remarked, but he wished to penetrate into his own intimacy, to explore his self in all its folds and creases, its "naturels plis." The reason, however, is not narcissistic. No self-indulgence here. Montaigne looks at himself as the only human reality he can observe with some accuracy, not as a unique and irreplaceable individual (as for instance Jean-Jacques Rousseau thought of himself), but as a reflection of the entire human condition. Yet even this closely examined self tends to elude him, for it is multifaceted, constantly evolving and mutating. Flux is indeed the great lesson. Human nature is multifarious and unstable. Life allows for no fixity. A terse formula sums up Montaigne's project: "I do not depict being. I depict passage." I have reread these words many times in my mind.

•   •   •

Rereading is subject to fortuitous circumstances, and remains a strictly personal affair. But the act of rereading, especially of books that have had a transformative effect, illustrates a wider common experience: the continuous shuttle, or to-and-fro movement, between art forms and lived life. It is a creative weaving, a process by which we are ceaselessly shaped. This to-and-fro motion between artifact and so-called reality takes various forms. It can occur between a given novel and specific urban setting, or between an admired painting and a geographic region. One might see the San Frediano district of Florence through a previous encounter with Vasco Pratolini's fiction, discover Saint Petersburg through exposure to Gogol and Dostoevsky, or grow fond of the Umbrian countryside through earlier views of the delicate trees in Perugino's landscape compositions.

Inevitably, this raises the question of sincerity. Are my perceptions of Piazza Navona and of Via Giulia not hopelessly colored by my readings of Stendhal's *Promenades dans Rome*? A steady exchange takes place between the books that have left their mark on us and the life we lead. How to be sure that our reaction is really our own? Is there not a constant interaction between viewing life through books one has read, and reading (and rereading) books through what one has personally experienced?

But if these questions provoke anxiety, it can be an anxiety that exhilarates, filling one with a sense of discovery which, as I recall, goes back to childhood. For long before the bookish intimacies of the pandemic confinement, the little boy I was, disobeying his parents' injunctions, used to read secretly at night, under the blanket with the aid of a flashlight, and understood even then, though only vaguely, that the book dear to him at that moment made it possible to see the world around him, himself included, in a new light.

Part III · The French Connection

9 · Lessons of Montaigne

Delightfully unpredictable, Michel de Montaigne seems to follow in his *Essays* a program of digressive spontaneity. Engaging in a dialogue with writers of antiquity and readers in the present, these essays, carrying titles that correspond only vaguely, if at all, to their fluid substance, are above all a provocative dialogue with himself. Or rather, they offer a conversation, in the original Latin sense of frequentation and keeping company. Montaigne the writer enjoys the close presence of Montaigne the person. In their exchanges, they do their best to avoid smugness and pedantry. The author of the *Essays* even takes pride in occasionally misquoting his sources. He often quotes from memory. Mental playfulness seems to be his intimate motto. He juggles ideas, and writes with the delight of a genuine *dilettante*.

What kind of person was this most unconventional philosopher who lived and wrote in the tormented times of religious wars during the second half of the sixteenth century? A wealthy landowner of possible Jewish Marrano origins, he was a respected local magistrate who became mayor of Bordeaux—a function his father had occupied. While still in his late thirties, he decided to retire from public life, settle on his estate, and spend his days in the tower of his château, amid the books of his library, engaged in intellectual commerce with his beloved writers of antiquity. Latin was in fact a language he spoke before French—the result of a decision of his father, who held very special views about his son's education and chose for him a German tutor who knew no French and communicated with him only in the language of Virgil and Cicero.

As a married man, later in life, Michel had very little interest in the duties of a husband. From his tower, he occasionally watched his wife busy at work in the courtyard or the garden. Surrounded by books, he far preferred observing himself read and think, often surprised by his own thoughts. Mental mobility became a central theme of his *Essays*. The first edition appeared in 1580. It was followed by other editions that included constantly added passages. In spite of his declared choice of a private existence in the company of great writers, he remained involved, at times secretly, in the agitated politics of his period. He had dealings with the ill-fated Henri III, who liked his *Essays*, and closer contact with Henri de Navarre, who became Henri IV, and who appreciated his advice.

What is this unusual collection and blend of textual commentary, philosophical observation, autobiographical detail, self-examination and self-contradiction that Montaigne chose to call "essays?" He himself refers to his work as a *fricassée*, a culinary term designating a stew, and by extension a concoction of diverse ingredients. Every essay carries a specific title, but hardly any one of them has a precise subject. Not one of them stands out because of its rigor or consistency. The discursive voice speaking to us carries on a protean discourse. And that voice speaks abundantly about himself. He admits that this "self" in its endless diversity is his real subject. The religious thinker Blaise Pascal, reading him closely and at times admiringly a century later, found reprehensible this dedication to his "hateful self" ("*moi haïssable*"). A century later still, Voltaire, reacting sharply to Pascal's austere Jansenist stricture, maintained that he was charmed by Montaigne's "*charmant projet*" to write so fully about himself.

It is difficult not to agree with Voltaire about Montaigne's captivating self-revelations. No detail about his own person seems insignificant to him or undeserving of being written about: his physical appearance, his speech defects and way of walking, his digestive problems, his sleeping habits, the kidney stones that caused him so much pain, his taste in food and wines. He knows himself, or believes he does. For he also discovers himself, and to a certain extent invents himself as he writes. The self he tries to describe remains in motion, and not always easy to capture. Toward the end of one of his richest essays, "Of the Art of Discussion," he sums up his efforts at self-portraiture: "I present myself standing and lying down, front and rear, on the right and left and in all my natural postures." In his program of sincerity, Montaigne also knows full well that his natural postures, his "*naturels plis*," are mobile, and surprise even himself.

And he surprises his reader by his provocative openness of mind and limitless curiosity. At the opening of one of his most celebrated essays, "Of Experience," he remarks that there is nothing more natural than the desire for knowledge. Montaigne's desire is, however, not satisfied by mere facts and affirmed certitudes. He relishes playing with ideas and delights in unsettling his reader and himself by challenging commonly held moral and intellectual convictions. His tolerance for views opposed to his own helps him revise his opinions: "No prepositions astonish me, no belief offends me, whatever contrast it offers with my own. There is no fancy so frivolous and so extravagant that it does not seem quite suitable to the production of the human spirit." These remarkable lines appear in the essay on the art of discussion ("De l'art de conferer").

In his final essay, "Of Experience," Montaigne outlines what amounts to a program of relativism, referring at the start to Aristotle and Epicurus: "Never did two men judge alike about the same thing, and it is impossible to find two opinions exactly alike, not only in different men, but in the same man at different times." Self-contradiction ultimately appears as a virtue. In the already mentioned essay on discussion, Montaigne insists that contradictions of opinion arouse and stimulate him ("m'éveillent seulement et m'excercent").

Charmed as he was by Montaigne's determination to reveal so much about himself, Voltaire might have insisted on the irresistible appeal of his style. Vigorous, sinuous, concrete, his way of writing comes with an oral quality that almost conveys physical gestures. Montaigne himself describes the kind of language he favors, both in speaking and on paper: "The speech I love is a simple, natural speech, the same on paper as in the mouth, a speech succulent and sinewy, brief and compressed, not so much dainty and well-combed, as vehement and brusque." To this telling passage appearing in his essay on the education of children Montaigne might have added that he does not object to coarse expressions when appropriate.

His way of expressing himself reflects his distaste for all conformities and rigid beliefs. Stubbornness, especially, offends him as a sure sign of unintelligence: "Obstinacy and heat of opinion are the surest proof of stupidity. Is there anything so certain, resolute, disdainful, contemplative, grave and serious as an ass?" Heat of opinion ("*ardeur d'opinion*") is assuredly not one of Montaigne's dispositions. He also shows little inclination to being "*grave et sérieux*" in the manner of the long-eared and coarse-maned quadruped he mentions. This kind of reprehensible gravity is totally unrelated to the lighthearted humanism displayed by Montaigne.

．　　．　　．

As a child, the future author of the *Essays* only heard his regional Perigord dialect spoken by the peasant family to which his father had entrusted him so he might learn how ordinary people live. A little later he heard and spoke Latin before he knew French. That, too, was his father's idea. Pierre Eyquem de Montaigne, as already mentioned, had very unusual plans for the education of his son, choosing a German tutor for him who did not speak French but was an excellent Latinist, so that young Michel and this tutor would communicate exclusively in Latin, both orally and in writing. This prepared the boy for close familiarity with writers of antiquity, proving directly relevant to the genesis of the *Essays*. Montaigne frequents the Stoics, the Epicureans, the Skeptics. He reads Seneca, Lucretius, Horace. From his early years on, he enjoys Ovid's poetic accounts of miraculous metamorphoses, the historical writings of Tacitus, Plutarch's biographies. And he has a taste for the poetry of Virgil.

In the early stages, he develops the habit of gathering quotations from classical authors, providing some personal comments. Collecting citations, aphorisms, maxims, and examples from the Greco-Roman heritage had been a popular genre during the Renaissance. Montaigne's originality from the start was to use the dialogue with the revered authors of the past largely as a pretext for entering into a dialogue with himself. In his essay "Of Solitude," he recommends that we reserve a back of the store all our own (*"une arrière boutique toute nostre"*) in order to keep up an ordinary conversation between us and ourselves. Such a conversation turns into an exercise in introspection. In another essay ("Of Presumption") he makes his point clearer:

> The world always looks straight ahead; as for me, I turn my gaze inward, I fix it there and I keep it busy. Everyone looks in front of self; as for me, I look inside of me; I have no business but with myself; I continually observe myself, I take stock of myself, I taste myself.

Montaigne knows fully well that this habit of introspection or self-auscultation in search of self-knowledge risks becoming his principal preoccupation. In his essay on the art of discussion he admits that intimacy with his self seems to be his central subject: "I dare not only speak of myself, but to speak only of myself." This dedication to a quasi-clinical self-observation is, however, not narcissistic. It functions in his case as a more general quest for insight into human thought and behavior. Referring to his own person, Montaigne tellingly resorts to philosophical and scientific language. The essay "Of Experience" takes off with the general statement that there is no more natural desire than the desire for knowledge. A few pages later, Montaigne makes perfectly clear how he personally envisages this inquiry: "I study myself more than any other subject. That is my metaphysics, that is my physics." And in pursuit of this self-observing, self-examining curriculum, the author of the *Essays* watches himself closely in his daily behavior. He even attempts to retain consciousness watching himself in his sleep. Toward the conclusion of the essay on experience, the ultimate essay of the collection, Montaigne recalls how he had asked to be awakened while sleeping and dreaming: "To the end that sleep itself should not escape me thus stupidly, at one time I saw fit to have mine disturbed, so that I might gain a glimpse of it."

The priority of self-awareness turns into an intellectual adventure. In the stimulating communication with himself, Montaigne relishes self-contradiction. He seems not to foresee his next move. This almost playful preoccupation with the "self" is, however, radically different from Jean-Jacques Rousseau's determination to talk about himself because, as Rousseau explains, there never was and never will be another Jean-Jacques Rousseau. In the second paragraph of his *Confessions*, Rousseau famously affirmed that he is made unlike anyone he has ever met. His claim to uniqueness goes to an even greater extreme: "I will venture to say that I am like no one in the world." The mold in which he was formed will be "broken."

Montaigne would have been exceedingly surprised by such exceptionalist views of one's own being—especially by Rousseau's statement that he is altogether different from others ("*je suis autre*"). In stark contrast to the self-proclaimed unique Jean-Jacques, Montaigne views the self that so occupies him as representative: "Every human being bears the entire form of the human condition," he writes in the essay "Of Repentance." Nothing could be more opposed to Rousseau's brand of egocentrism. Attentive self-observation is for Montaigne the first step of a broader heuristic inquiry into ever mobile human thought and behavior. But the self is what he can know best—not as he is or was, but in the act of living and becoming, or even in the act of becoming Montaigne by writing the *Essays*.

·   ·   ·

Montaigne's brand of humanism inevitably concerns itself with the education of the young. Books, yes—but please, no servitude to the authors' opinions. One of his essays concerns itself in large part with the education of children. They should learn joyously, without being oppressed by pedants and pedantry, or by the tyrannical constraints of the rulers of "rhetoric." The question of education comes up in other essays, as does the disdain for prescriptive lessons of speech. "I would rather have my son learn to speak in the taverns than in the schools of fine speech" ("*escoles de la parlerie*"). The child's mind must not be cluttered. Tutors should see to it that their pupils cultivate a well-developed brain ("*une tête bien faite*") rather than a stuffed one. All knowledge must be examined and then digested, not blindly taken in, to be later regurgitated. All opinions must be questioned, never dumbly accepted. What strikes a fresh, perhaps even a new note in this skeptical approach to learning, is the far-reaching resistance to all doctrinaire authority, the stress on individual mental agility, on weighing ideas and concepts, on developing curiosity and openness of mind.

The art of thinking necessarily implies the art of living. Montaigne's suspicious attitude toward doctors of medicine, his questioning their authoritative prescriptions, signal a quite special preoccupation with health. And for good reason. He suffered repeatedly from painful kidney stones. Self-diagnosis and self-planned therapy also serve moral well-being. Montaigne travels all the way to Lucca in Tuscany for special baths to treat his chronic condition. This preoccupation with health and distrust of doctors as well as remedies does not, however, indicate hypochondria. Rather, it speaks to his greater trust in nature ("*se commettre à nature*" is one of his favorite expressions), and to his belief that there is wisdom in learning to live with what the flesh is heir to. The awareness of mortality must not translate into fear of life. During a lengthy convalescence, after a fall from a horse that almost killed him, Montaigne understood that living, as he put it, was his real business.

He had learned in pain and distress that life was too precious to live in dread of losing it. Life had to be savored to the last drop. It was all we had ("*c'est notre tout*"). Acceptance of all that comes also means making the most of it. In his last essay, Montaigne sums it up: "Our great and glorious masterpiece is to live appropriately" ("*vivre à propos*"). This sense of acceptance and harmonic moderation comes close to the ancient Greek notion of *metron ariston*—the excellence of good measure. Montaigne's view of life ultimately presents itself as a form of Epicureanism heightened by a sharp personal awareness of flux and impermanence.

• • •

Modern readers of Montaigne may feel that the *Essays* project, ahead of their time, the image of an author who sees himself and his fellow creatures as both mutable and self-shaping. For we are, each one of us, in motion and changing ("*ondoyant et divers*"). Humans cannot be defined, but discover and reveal themselves in the act of living, much as Montaigne discovers, or rather creates Montaigne in the act of writing the *Essays*. "I do not portray being. I portray passage" ("*Je ne peints pas l'estre. Je peints le passage*"), he declares in the first paragraph of the essay on repentance. This notion of flux and becoming may remind readers today of existentialist views of human freedom and unpredictability: "Not only do I find it hard to link our actions with one another, but each one separately I find hard to designate properly by some principal characteristic, so two-sided and motley do they seem in different lights" ("Of Experience"). But these multiple ambiguities and discontinuities of human behavior only incite Montaigne to pursue his ceaseless exploration of his own thoughts and actions. "There is no end to our researches," he remarks in the same essay. Judging our most ordinary moves as loaded with often conflicting meanings is perhaps the most modern aspect of Montaigne, who appears little drawn to unambiguous heroic deeds and extreme situations. Transcendental humors and vertiginous heights, he himself admits, are not to his taste. They frighten him. Conversely, holding ourselves in contempt he considers a terrible affliction. The pride of being fully human implies learning a lesson in moderation and modesty. One of Montaigne's most endearing observations appears at the conclusion of his final essay, and ends with a crude French word. Just after reminding the reader that when walking on stilts we must still walk on our legs, Montaigne adds, "And on the loftiest throne in the world, we are still sitting only on our ass" ("*sus nostre cul*").

10 · The Audacities of Molière's Don Juan

Don Juan seduces and perturbs. The elements of his legend are rich in glamour: his amorous conquests, his insolent pride, his defiance of the living and the dead, his special notion of freedom, his encounter with the marble statue, his determination and courage in facing his destiny. Every one of his moves is at the same time captivating and transgressive.

If the legendary figure of Don Juan challenges all moral norms, Molière's play *Dom Juan ou le Festin de Pierre* (1665) transcends and violates the aesthetic criteria of his period. This subversive comedy is hardly funny; it offends accepted dramatic rules through the disjointed and arbitrary nature of its episodes: a chance encounter in a Sicilian town with a woman the Spanish seducer abandoned, the seduction of two peasant girls near the seashore, a philosophic conversation with his superstitious valet in an unnamed forest, a combat with armed bandits, a blaspheming discussion with a pious beggar who refuses to be bribed into cursing—episodes that, without any apparent logical link, nonetheless lead Don Juan with inevitability to the marble statue of the Commander he killed, and then straight into the flames of Hell.

Different theatrical traditions clash in Molière's play, as do characters who do not come from the same world: a farcical servant, noble Spaniards in search of vengeance, a bourgeois merchant trying to cash in on a debt, a specter, an ambulant statue carrying out Heaven's punishment. Dissonance sets the tone. Grand and grandiloquent diction alternate with brisk staccato effects that seem to announce the ironic recitativi of Mozart's *Don Giovanni* (the librettist of the opera, Lorenzo Da Ponte, surely took a good look at Molière's version of the legend).

Banal contrivances of the commedia dell'arte are raised to the level of high comedy and troubling insights. Buffooneries and claptrap lead to critical comments. Everything seems meant to disconcert. Not the least baffling is the gluttonous and superstitious servant Sganarelle, tied to the depraved nobleman by a blend of fascination and fear, and who is entrusted by the playwright with the task of defending religion.

The most disconcerting is of course Don Juan himself. Is Molière's seducer also a thinker; is this sensualist a skeptic philosopher? He is a conqueror uninterested in his conquest, faithless in every sense of the word (is he not also an infidel?) but determinedly faithful to himself. Paradoxes show up at every point. His affirmation of life turns into a negation. This mocker of religious beliefs in the supernatural invites a speaking statue to supper. And what is one to make of Molière's astonishing decision to have the proud nobleman give magisterial lessons in the art of hypocrisy to his stupefied valet?

One imagines the perplexities of both actor and director. How to play the part? Is Don Juan above all a voluptuary? Is he coldhearted, perhaps even cruel? Should the performer stress his ironic tone, his sense of superiority? Is the depraved nobleman a performing artist in his very delinquencies, a supreme dilettante in quest of delicate sensations? Is he what at the time was called an *esprit fort*—a doubter of religious truths, or even an atheist in disguise? Should the actor interpret his role as a romantic reincarnation of the great Fallen One? Is he disenchanted, somber, blasé? Or should he be conceived as perpetually carefree, pirouetting though life with style and insensitivity?

The opening signals of the play already point to the problematic nature of Molière's Don Juan. He does not answer but unloads one question after another, just as later in the play he will almost unfailingly dodge accountability by making the others speak while he remains evasive. When he first appears, in scene two, his quick interrogative utterances reveal a fundamental silence, a typical refusal of any true dialogue, an aggressive elusiveness: "Who was just talking to you?"—"How long has he been in this city?"—"And what business brings him here?"—"And what did you say to him?"—"What do you make of this affair?"

Literary history does not elucidate the many questions that surround Molière's version of the seducer's legend. The Spanish dramatist Tirso di Molina is credited with being the first, around 1630, to publish a play on the amorous exploits and outrageous delicts of the famous libertine,

El burlador de Sevilla y convidado de piedra (*The Trickster of Seville and the Stone Guest*)—a baroque composition tracing an unsavory path from crime and debauchery to an edifying ultimate repentance. From Spain the legend transited to Italy, where the commedia dell'arte transformed it by stuffing it with gross buffooneries. From Italy it moved to France with versions that were surely known to Molière. His play, however, remains unique in its daring philosophical implications.

Over the years, the myth of Don Juan has tempted countless writers and musicians: Goldoni wrote a tragicomedy; Mozart created his *Don Giovanni* in which the delicate music of the minuet is suddenly transformed into tragic orchestrations of threats and superhuman defiance; Alexander Pushkin composed *Kamenny Gost* (*The Stone Guest*). The list, like that of Leporello's catalogue, goes on: Alexandre Dumas, José Zorilla, Nikolaus Lenau, Richard Strauss. For centuries, the great Seducer has intrigued and infused the European imagination: Théophile Gautier, Leo Tolstoy, Barbey d'Aurevilly, George Bernard Shaw, Henry de Montherlant, Max Frisch . . . And there is more.

·   ·   ·

But what is Don Juan? Is he the supreme hedonist? Does the great lover try to forget an old wound? Or rather than oblivion, does he seek an impossible, unattainable love? Does he fear entrapment in immobility, or on the contrary is he haunted by the erosive work of time and the misery of aging? Molière's protagonist is explicit on some of these fears. He dismisses fidelity because it would mean "burying oneself forever," being "dead" while still in one's youthful years. Does the traditional Don Juan seek amorous conquests, as well as perpetual feasting and wining (celebrated in Mozart's brilliant aria "Fin ch'han dal vino"), as a haughty negation of quotidian boredom and banality? Does he perchance dream of purity, of pure love? Or is he merely a carnal adventurer in search of virgin territories, whose predominant passion, as the servant Leporello explains, is the young beginner, "*la giovin principiante*"? Is the legendary Spaniard endowed with a boundless appetite, a "*barbaro appetito*" that appalls his envious servant? A more exalting, heroic account is perhaps in order, and Don Juan, far from being a mere sensualist, displays the highest qualities of courage—the courage of a desperate and ultimately hopeless struggle against a transcendent order.

Molière's very singular Don Juan remains of course the serial lover and the serial betrayer. Sganarelle calls his master an "*épouseur à toutes mains*," a man ready to "espouse" any female at any time and then abandon her. Nothing is too hot or too cold for him, too old or too young: young damsels, ladies, bourgeois city dwellers, peasant girls. His amorous voraciousness corresponds to his other appetites. But Molière does not insist on this erotic eclecticism. His Don Juan is not really the slave of a lascivious temperament. From the start, he appears as an artist of love, a connoisseur of delicate sensations. His eye takes note of the slightest nuances and transforms the desired other into a provocative spectacle. The active and performing seducer is at the same time an appreciative spectator.

These pleasures of the mind and the senses, these delights in cerebral eroticism, are not devoid of a certain cruelty. Molière's Don Juan is also an artist in wickedness. His essential immorality is clearly stated by his servant, even before his first appearance: "a great lord turned evil is a terrible thing." His own father, whom he in so many words wishes to see dead, goes so far as to call him to his face a "monster."

The father's grandiloquent tirade denouncing his son's immorality remains, however, somewhat vacuous and off the point. Molière's Don Juan is much more than a morally corrupt aristocrat. Even his wickedness, his *méchanceté*, is a form of playacting. But aesthetic and ethical notions are not easily compatible. Desire and moral freedom come into conflict. Can freedom exist where desire reigns? Desire can fetter and impede freedom. This conflict is in fact at the psychological and philosophical core of the Don Juan myth, and no one has understood it better than Molière. The word "philosophy" shows up, though in a comical context, in the play's first sentence: "Whatever Aristotle and all of philosophy might say . . ." And it is not by chance that Sganarelle says of his dialectically gifted master that he speaks "like a book." His rhetorical skills unsettle his interlocutors. And when he artfully mimics the style of contemporary bigots and hypocrites, shocking Sganarelle with his unexpected "devilish style" ("diable de style"), it is clear that Molière has shifted from the tone of comedy and farce to a strategy of subversion and polemical attack.

For Molière evidently uses the figure of Don Juan to get back at his doctrinaire enemies of the *cabale des dévots* who had denounced his *Le Tartuffe*, a play about a supreme hypocrite indulging, under cover of religious piety, in parasitism and lechery. This dogmatic cabal had only recently succeeded in having anyone performing or attending this play excommunicated. In composing the play about Don Juan, Molière was thus provoked into espousing audacities that echo freethinking, and mostly clandestine (because dangerous) intellectual currents of the time. As the play progresses, his amorous adventurer sound increasingly like a bold adventurer in the realm of subversive thought, a *libertin* in the two senses of the word—sensuous and hostile to religious pieties. The audacity of Don Juan turns out to display Molière's own audacity. This audacious *libertinage*, a subversive seduction of the mind, takes the form of aggressive disbelief, even downright atheism.

As of the beginning of act 3, Don Juan clearly appears as a derisive logician. But it is obvious that the playwright himself is the ironic dialectician. A remarkable dialogue between the skeptical master and the superstitious servant about the "miracles" of medicine stresses the antireligious meaning of libertinage:

> SGANARELLE What! Sir! You are an unbeliever in medicine also?
> DON JUAN It is one of the greatest errors entertained by mankind.
> SGANARELLE What! You don't believe in senna, cassia, and in emetic wine?
> DON JUAN And why do you want me to believe in them?
> SGANARELLE You have a really impious soul. But you cannot deny that for some time now this emetic wine has made some famous noise. Its miracles have converted the most incredulous minds.

The key words of this passage about medicine—unbeliever, believe, soul, impious, converted, incredulous—clearly belong to the religious lexicon and point to Don Juan's disbelief in matters of religion. But they also serve to conceal Molière's own thoughts, as he seems to disapprove and approve at the same time, while not so secretly siding with the character who should be proven wrong yet seems to make sense.

This dialogue is not the only example of subversive rationalism. When Sganarelle reminds his master that one must not make light of the "sacred mystery" of marriage, the response comes briskly: "Enough of that. It's an issue between Heaven and me, and we will settle it well without your help." Don Juan openly mocks his servant's beliefs and nonsensical arguments. When Sganarelle asks the great seducer if he believes in the afterlife, the answer comes in a triple burst of laughter. This mocking denial of an otherworldly reality prepares the audience and the reader for his bravado in inviting the statue of the Commander to supper—an invitation confirming his insolent courage. At the end, he shows himself proudly incapable of repentance.

Even his pretended defense of hypocrisy is an act of defiance. It also reveals Molière's complicity with his protagonist. Don Juan's satirical sortie against the cabal of hypocrites—the *cabale des dévots*—is clearly directed against Molière's enemies who had denounced his *Le Tartuffe* to the powerful religious authorities. The length and audacity of this speech about the advantages of hypocrisy leaves no doubt as to Molière's personal investment in this oblique attack against those who had almost succeeded in having him excommunicated. His boldness was quickly perceived. Don Juan, pretending to have discovered the art of imposture, explains the benefits of the hypocrite's vocation. By devout mummery one can, he says, silence everybody, and commit any crime with impunity.

. . .

It has been objected that, in having Don Juan praise hypocrisy, Molière went against the logic of the personage, that it was not consistent with his loyalty to himself, with his determination, as he himself says, to show that nothing can "shake" ("*ébranler*") him, not even the arrival of the statue. But Don Juan is also playful, and the digression on hypocrisy is not incompatible with his ludic temperament. He is used to playing roles. Far from being duplicitous and tartuffish, he shares Molière's courage. Don Juan the accused becomes an audacious accuser. His pride, his arrogance, his disdain for all that is banal, demand an ironic and playacting distance between himself and the world outside him.

This playful distance is similar to that of a theatrical performance. The great seducer's theatrical imitation of the hypocrite (etymologically the word means "actor" in Greek) provides him with the artistic delights of what he himself ironically calls a respected "art." It is with great satisfaction that he practices his new role ("Heaven ordains it"—"Heaven wishes it so"—"I obey the voice of Heaven"). Never has Don Juan had more fun, or been more entertained by the gullibility of others.

Molière was severely criticized, even violently attacked, for mocking religious virtue. The harsh indictment by one Sieur Richemont is worth recording: "Molière—who makes fun of God and of the Devil, who mocks heaven and hell, who mixes things up, who confuses virtue and vice, who believes and does not believe, who cries and who laughs, who reproves and approves, who is a censor and an atheist, a hypocrite and a libertine, who is all at once a human being and a demon, a devil in the flesh." This vituperative reaction is no doubt excessive, but shows to what extent the play was perturbing at the time. Even more moderate views indicate that Molière's audacious attack on religious hypocrisy was disquieting to his contemporaries.

The figure of Don Juan as conceived by Molière is of course troubling in other ways. On a psychological level, what is one to make of this obsession with "freedom," of this entrapment in mobility and change? And how to respond to this rebellion against society's moral order that leads to the confrontation with a statue representing timeless justice?

The ambiguities of the play also point to its modernity. Playful speculation and spinning circular discourse (babbling Sganarelle falls on his buttocks, dizzied by his own words) foreshadow the theatrical world of a Samuel Beckett and the "theater of the absurd." They are also symptomatic of a culture increasingly haunted by its own negations. Molière's achievement is to have communicated the disarray when moral codes and moral values are challenged, to have given dramatic expression to ideas considered dangerous at the time, and to have exposed himself courageously to the danger of seeming to espouse them.

11 · The Bitterness of Candide

Doctor Pangloss, young Candide's tutor, has the same answer to every question about life: "This is the best of all possible worlds." His disciples sing this reassuring lesson in joyful unison in Leonard Bernstein's musical version of Voltaire's text, even though all of them are bound to experience a full measure of the miseries the world has to offer. The lyrics of the work (its final version written by a number of hands, but chiefly by the poet Richard Wilbur and Bernstein himself) basically follow the plot of the famous tale. Bernstein's singing protagonists roam through the Old and the New World, and they witness and suffer all possible calamities: battlefield massacres, rapes and disembowelments, disfiguring venereal maladies, inquisitional tortures, floggings and maimings—even shipwrecks and earthquakes. They themselves participate in a range of turpitudes—debauchery, prostitution, greed, and murder. Yet in this basically sunny musical work, everything leads to a song.

These songs are glittering, witty, satirical, parodistic, evoking diverse musical styles, including those of the operatic tradition. Key lines of the arias and group numbers display an ironic lightheartedness: "Life is happiness indeed," "Oh, happy we!," "What a perfect day for hanging!," "Glitter and be gay," "We could dance on eggs." The duet "Life Is Happiness Indeed," sung by Candide and Cunégonde after the opening chorale, looks forward to joyful horseback riding and books to read. This early love duet conjures up a blissful existence on a luxurious yacht and in aristocratic marble residences, with costume balls and smiling babies, faithful servants, and faithful dogs. They plan to live exclusively in "luxury and stylish charm." At the end of their transcontinental travails and torments, their outlook becomes more modest. They hope to build an ordinary house, chop their wood, make their garden grow. It is a blander, disenchanted form of happiness. But happiness is still the tune. As the curtain is about to fall on Bernstein's brilliant work, the couple has learned that life is "neither bad nor good." Still, they intend to find a measure of happiness, even if tinged with a faint taste of bitterness.

•   •   •

Yet the mood of disenchantment ("We'll do the best we know") that accompanies the final notes of Bernstein's musical version is far removed from the mordant irony and unredeemable bitterness of Voltaire's subversive tale denouncing the tyranny of both Church and State—a tale that was quickly denounced as heretical, banned, and put on the Vatican's Index of Prohibited Books. When *Candide* appeared in 1759, Voltaire was probably the most notorious (and controversial) public intellectual. He knew the personal risks he was taking. He had the work published as the anonymous translation of a nonexistent German author, identified as Dr. Ralph. To be accused of heresy and religious blasphemy was still exceedingly dangerous in the so-called enlightened eighteenth-century.

Voltaire (1694–1778) is surely the most vocal, the wittiest, and also the most intolerant of the philosophers committed to the struggle against intolerance: A steadfast defender of the persecuted, he swamped all of Europe under the propaganda barrage of pamphlets and letters. His correspondence alone occupies dozens of volumes. He is responsible for some of the most biting tales and novelettes in verse as well as in prose. Their light touch, however, should not deceive the reader. Voltaire meant serious business.

The seriousness underlying the surface lightheartedness is perfectly illustrated from the outset by a passage in the first chapter describing young Cunégonde's eye-opening experience as she surprises Dr. Pangloss copulating with the family servant Paquette: "she saw Doctor Pangloss behind some bushes giving a lesson in experimental physics [physique expérimentale] to her mother's maid, a pretty little brunette who seemed very teachable. As Cunégonde had a great interest in science, she watched the experiment being repeated with breathless interest. She saw clearly the Doctor's sufficient reason [raison suffisante], observing both the cause and effect." The passage is characteristic. The deliberate understatement, the complicitous smile elicited by the licentious undertones, the ironic treatment of eroticism, all suit the taste of the period. But there is more to it. Voltaire's stylish licentiousness hides another purpose. His reference to a sex act as "physique expérimentale" is bound to tickle the reader who has been informed that Doctor Pangloss teaches "métaphysico-théologico-cosmolonigologie." Linguistically, it also discredits the Panglosses of this world by ridiculing their philosophical jargon. The anatomical "sufficient reason" that Cunégonde admires, as well as the terms "cause" and "effect," clearly have in the context nothing in common with the didactic uses to which they are normally put. All this leads to the bitter reality of the real cause and effect. At the end of chapter 3, we learn about the results of the repeated experiments with the chambermaid behind the bushes: Pangloss's horribly pustulous face, half-rotted nose, black teeth, and other syphilitic lesions and symptoms—none of which discourages him from repeating that all is for the best in the best of possible worlds.

Almost perversely, Voltaire piles up pseudocomical incidents to convey his indignation and anger: Candide flogged in cadence with the religious anthem at the auto-da-fé; opposing armies singing fervent Te Deums before the battle; the slow roasting of human flesh offered as a spectacle to ladies being served refreshments; Cunégonde shared as a concubine by a rich Jew and a powerful Inquisitor; an old woman whose left buttock is cut off to provide meals; apes running after girls to nibble their behinds (a seeming obsession with that part of the anatomy); repeated accounts of rapes; innumerable deaths and burlesque resurrections leading to new calamities. After having been hanged and then cut open, Pangloss returns to life and calmly resumes teaching his absurd optimistic doctrine. Cunégonde's brother is killed twice, and twice comes back to life, while Cunégonde herself, though raped and disemboweled by Bulgar soldiers, continues her amorous adventures. As to promiscuous Paquette, she is miraculously cured of the venereal disease she communicated to Pangloss and turns up in Venice, sprightly and natty, in the company of Brother Giroflée, a philandering member of a religious congregation. But this grotesque comedy of resuscitations is hardly cheerful, leaving the reader with the uncomfortable feeling that the author brings his characters back to life only to have them robbed, betrayed, flogged, raped, and disemboweled once again.

The lightness of touch as well as the preposterous nature of the narrative heightens the horror of the situations. Voltaire's rapier is so sharp, his thrusts are so dexterous, that by the time the wound begins to hurt, the double-edged blade is already cutting elsewhere. The transition from comedy to the ugliest reality is often rapid and brutal. About the pleasures of warfare, for instance: "Nothing was as beautiful, as light, as brilliant, as well ordered as the two armies. The trumpets, the fifes, the oboes, the drums, the canons, produced such a harmony . . ." But what a harmony! As Voltaire explains, it is the harmony of hell. Thousands of "heroes" are swiftly eliminated from this best of worlds by those canons, while the bayonet becomes the sufficient reason that helps another few thousands out of their bliss. Voltaire's tone abruptly changes as he depicts the horrors of warfare: death, pillage, destruction. Wherever Candide looks, the ground is strewn with dismembered limbs and spilled brains.

These brusque modulations occur on almost every page. Issachar, the old choleric Jew who shares Cunégonde with the Inquisitor, appears at first as a comic figure. But let him die (Candide kills both the Inquisitor and the Jew), and the Inquisitor is buried in a splendid church, while the body of the Jew is thrown on a refuse-dump. Voltaire does not miss a single occasion to make the most repugnant point.

There is indeed, some may find, a deliberate nastiness in this tale, and even a kind of pleasure in this nastiness, as its author depicts one calamity after another. The characters themselves seem to compete with one another, pretending to have suffered more than anyone else. Cunégonde is amused and indignant when old Abigail claims to have known greater miseries than she has:

> "My dear Abigail, unless you have been raped twice by two Bulgars, received two knife stabs in your belly, had two of your castles destroyed, two mothers and two fathers beheaded, and watched two of your lovers flogged in an auto-da-fé, I do not see how you can have had it worse than I, especially since I was born a baroness."

But of course Abigail is the daughter of a pope, and a pope, even for Voltaire, is slightly more eminent than a German baron. Abigail will, moreover, partially succeed in outdoing Cunégonde. And just like his characters who indulge in this grotesque competition, so also Voltaire strives to outdo himself, as though determined to test how, from chapter to chapter, he can paint an even blacker picture of the human condition, as though driven by a compulsion to squelch the remnants of a lingering illusion.

Pet grudges and pet hatreds come into sharp relief. It is with obvious delight that Voltaire has the tribe of Oreillons shout, while their cauldron is heating, "It's a Jesuit, a Jesuit! . . . let's eat some Jesuit!" Voltaire's private cauldron, one might say, is constantly boiling, as he himself feasts, not only on Jesuits, but on intriguing and lecherous monks, persecuting priests, cruel Inquisitors, and delirious theologians, all of whom he devours with boundless appetite. Organized religion in general provokes his ire. Even the Bible is not spared. Candide refers disparagingly to "that big book," belonging to the ship's captain, which tells the story of creation. To the inevitable question of why this world was created at all, the gloomy answer comes swiftly: "To make us mad" ("pour nous faire enrager").

Voltaire's gloom extends beyond Church and religion. It is as though he were determined to compete with all the turpitudes, all the human-made and natural disasters, and tried singlehandedly to outdo with his pen the horrors of the Lisbon earthquake which, on November 1, 1755, as he was about to write *Candide*, had sent shockwaves throughout Europe. This cataclysmic event, with its deadly tsunami, occurred on All Saints' Day, which encouraged preachers to attribute the seismic catastrophe to God's wrath against the sinful Portuguese. The city lay in ruins, with an estimated thirty thousand or more victims. Voltaire's personal shock at the news provoked him immediately into composing his incendiary *Poem on the Disaster of Lisbon* (1756), a scornful attack against philosophies of optimism (such as that of Gottfried Leibniz) and theological trust in Providence.

The seismic calamity of 1775 soon also fed into *Candide*, but this time Voltaire communicated more than somber musings about blind natural forces of destruction. He was out to denounce chiefly human cruelty and human indifference to suffering. Yet behind his somber message, and the accumulated examples of atrocities, one can easily perceive an implicit ethics of solidarity.

If *Candide* may seem repetitive in places, it is not that Voltaire, at the age of sixty-five, had lost his deft touch, but rather that it is precisely through trivializing repetition and unheroic tragedy that he achieves his desired effects. To make suffering impressive and tragic is already to exalt it, and thus almost to justify it. This is the last thing Voltaire wished to do. The Black slave with a leg and a hand missing, lying at the side of the road in tropical Surinam, is Voltaire's living symbol of suffering, and not some heroic figure who, even in his downfall, might vindicate the apparent absurdity of his fate. Voltaire accumulates unrelated, unjustified, and clearly unjustifiable suffering. He tells us through Martin, the character in the tale who stands for radical pessimism, that he knows of no town that does not hope for the destruction of the neighboring town, of no family that does not want to exterminate another family.

This unending survey of human misery has innocent Candide fall into a "black melancholy." No consolation is to be found in either philosophy or religion. When he asks the famous dervish ("the best philosopher in Turkey") why there is so much evil on the face of the earth, the answer comes in the form of a parable: "When His Highness sends a ship to Egypt, does he worry whether the ship's mice are comfortable or not?"

·   ·   ·

The reader of *Candide* feels thrust into a world of nastiness and darkness, quite devoid of the exuberant charm of the songs and lyrics in Bernstein's musical version. It is as though Voltaire, not content with undermining the Leibnizian theory of optimism (in which he shrewdly perceived a surreptitious return to theology), was determined to destroy any vestige of an illusion. It is bad enough that the world, according to his tale, is filled with scoundrels, that goodness does not pay, that God and nature are indifferent to human suffering. Even the few feelings that might brighten the picture a little, the feelings of love that sustain Candide in his search for Cunégonde, even those are poisoned by Voltaire's misanthropic mood. Early in the story, Cunégonde already betrays Candide; she follows Abigail's advice to remain the concubine of a Spanish nobleman who sports a comically long name, while poor Candide has to flee to safety. Voltaire further debunks the traditional love story, when finally Candide is granted the long-delayed reunion, by transforming Cunégonde into a weather-beaten hag with bloodshot eyes, scaly elbows, and the temper of a shrew. Small wonder that Candide no longer desires her, and marries her against his will.

Thrust pure and innocent into the world (as his name implies), Candide encounters all possible evils. Happiness and virtue are conceivable only in Eldorado, a utopian never-never land he enters as if in a dream, where greed and crime are unknown and all the inhabitants are kind and welcoming. Only it is a land that does not exist, a land of fantasy, "where nobody can go."

Readers may at some point wonder if *Candide* is just a somber joke, if Voltaire's sardonic snicker conveys an ironic (and hopeless) view of the human condition. But irony, even of the bitter kind, is by its very nature deceptive; it demands to be deciphered. This decoding of irony is especially required of some of the most influential texts of the period. Some of the most morally committed, most earnest, and also most controversial writings of the eighteenth century come in the form of witty tales, or philosophical dialogues, enhanced by perplexing sallies. Important issues typically appear in this guise, especially if they challenge Church and State, for wit and irony allow risk-taking authors to communicate, under the mask of sheer entertainment, the dangerous ideas they hold dear. Voltaire is a virtuoso of this ironic kind of philosophical dialogue: "Hey there, Mr. Savage! Do you believe, down there in Guinea, that we should burn people who don't share our opinions?—Surely! Provided you eat them." The very absurdity of the answer conveys an important lesson. Voltaire was fond of saying that a hanged man is of use to nobody. But no argument, no demonstration could convey as succinctly as the savage's answer the odious futility of murdering people to repress supposed heresies. There is something eminently unanswerable in the blunt words: "Provided you eat them."

Voltaire's practice of what the Parisian existentialists, two centuries later, would call *littérature engagée* was by no means determined exclusively by contemporary events such as the murderous persecution of Protestants or the Lisbon disaster. His many years of research as a social and cultural historian—culminating in the *Essay on Universal History, the Manners and Spirit of Nations* (1756), a prolonged dive into the past of countries, races, and religion—had convinced him that history, so far, was not much of a credit to the human species. He was struck by the seemingly endless, ubiquitous unfolding of violent events, of massacres, merciless tyrannies, and religious intolerance. So far at least.

But what about the future? There was some hope, maybe—if only humanity could be enlightened by science and reason. Voltaire was perhaps, in his own way, a kind of optimist after all. This side of his personality is mirrored, in the otherwise gloomy pages of *Candide*, by the counterpoint of a narrative that repeatedly hints at the possibility of a positive outlook. The sarcastic account of war is to be read as an indictment of "heroic" butcheries traditionally glorified in epic poems since antiquity, but this antimilitaristic and antiheroic indictment also implies the loftier ideal of pacifism. As for the imaginary land of Eldorado, it elicits the author's sad laughter because that utopian world does not exist. The listed virtues of Eldorado's inhabitants only remind us of the vices and crimes of the real world. Yet the description of Eldorado unfolds a blueprint for a truly civilized society—one that is scientifically minded, tolerant, and ruled by reason. A priest-free society with such love of justice that neither judges nor prisons are necessary. But above all, beyond the mocking laughter, there is the haunting dream of tolerance, the old dream that Voltaire was to project most explicitly and most tenderly in the closing paragraphs of his *Treatise on Tolerance* (1763)—very moving paragraphs written in the form of a prayer.

This prayer for tolerance and justice crowns the author's vehement denunciation of prejudice and religious fanaticism. The immediate references are to the persecution of Protestants, the atrocities of religious wars, and the tyrannical regimes that encourage hatred. Not surprisingly, the work had to be published outside of France, in Geneva; and it was quickly banned, while enjoying immediate popular success. Its central message was summed up in the concluding prayer, which extends well beyond a condemnation of religious bigotry and ideological violence. It expresses Voltaire's deism, as well as his hope for a better future.

You have not given us a heart to hate each other, nor hands to strangle each other.

Have all men remember that they are brothers. Implant in their hearts the same horror of tyranny.

This concluding prayer has resonated across the centuries. Two hundred and fifty years later, just after the January 2015 shootings in the editorial room of *Charlie Hebdo*, the magazine that had provocatively published satirical cartoons of the Prophet Muhammad, the *Treatise on Tolerance* was resurrected and became again a publishing sensation in France.

Irony, not prayer, however, was Voltaire's chief instrument, as illustrated by the corrosive bite of *Candide*—a work in which indignation hides a warm-hearted message. Irony does not want to be believed; it asks to be understood. The bitterness of the tale proves to be deceptive. For can it be truthfully said that there is no warmth in it? Candide's tears as he stares at the mutilated Black slave lying at the roadside are revealing. Weeping, he looks at the suffering man, and then, with tears still in his eyes, he pursues his way. Those tears of Candide, one suspects, may well be metaphorically Voltaire's own. They surely are symptomatic of a compassionate sensibility underlying the incisive wit of the narrative. Like many an apparent pessimist or misanthrope, Voltaire was at the core neither a cynic nor a disparager of humankind. His account of Candide's hard education betrays at crucial points that he feels pain at the pain of others and is outraged by injustice and cruelty. By negative examples, the work proclaims the need to protect human dignity, to value life, to reject hopelessness. But love of life does not mean self-love and indifference to others. Voltaire was well aware that he had no reason to complain based on his own personal fate. His bitterness remains a generous bitterness. Not everyone has recognized this. Jean-Jacques Rousseau, dismayed by Voltaire's poem on the Lisbon earthquake, accused him of indulging in detestable recriminations. He sent him a disapproving letter: "Sir, satisfied with glory, you live in the midst of wealth and abundance. Secure in your fame, you philosophize peacefully on the nature of the soul, and if your body ails, you have a private physician— and yet you see only evil in the world." What Rousseau did not know, or failed to understand, is that Voltaire was perfectly aware of his personal comfort—which made him even more keenly conscious of the suffering of others. "Except for my health, I am so happy that I am ashamed of it," he writes in May 1756. Voltaire knew that it was only too easy to be pleased with the world if one is pleased with one's lot. He was never guilty of such smugness.

This disposition to remain scandalized by the pain of others, this ever-renewed surprise in the face of recurring evil, suggest that perhaps the real Candide is Voltaire himself. "My dear master," says Candide's servant Cacambo, "you are always surprised by everything." Cacambo's

observation applies as well to Voltaire himself. And if Voltaire, at the age
of sixty-five, continued to be surprised, if he refused to become the accomplice of those who find it easy to bear with equanimity the suffering
of others, it is because, in spite of age and experience, he was still suffi-
ciently warm-hearted, honest, and courageous to find every evil shocking and every abuse detestable enough to provoke his generous anger.

12 · Encounters with Monsieur Beyle

My affair with Stendhal began in 1950 in Rome where, as a newlywed Fulbright scholar, I was doing research on his writings about Italy and working on my doctoral dissertation dealing with his peculiar brand of narrative irony. During that year in Rome, Bettina and I would often walk up the Janiculum hill, always stopping, as I love to recall, at the church of San Pietro in Montorio. Every time we reached that place, I could not avoid thinking about the enchanting overture to Stendhal's autobiographic *Life of Henry Brulard*, where he describes finding himself near the same church, perhaps standing exactly where we were standing, surveying the vast panorama of Rome. He could distinguish Monte Albano at a great distance and, closer to him, across the Tiber, the monuments of the Eternal City—a historical panorama that merged in his mind with the shifting panorama of his own life so enmeshed in recent history. Memory and historic events are thus at the same time collective and personal in those magical opening pages.

My initial discovery of Stendhal, some years earlier, was somehow linked to a nostalgia for an Italy as yet unknown to me. I imagined shimmering bays and promontories concealing mysterious grottoes. The first book by Stendhal that I came across was not, as might be expected, *The Red and the Black*, the novel about the passionate and ambitious young Julien Sorel. Nor was it a book on a reading list of any course I took as an undergraduate. The novel that dazzled me, and that I discovered on my own, was *The Charterhouse of Parma*. Even now that I have visited every nook of this novel, having reread and taught it a number of times, its very title, especially in French—*La Chartreuse de Parme*—gives me shivers of delight. The titles of certain books evoke a whole mental world, vistas of places one wishes to know, whiffs of desires. What I conjure up, when I read or hear the syllables of Stendhal's Italian novel, is a very special quality of autumnal light. The day is reaching its end; a few translucid clouds enhance the sky, while distant hills are brought into painterly relief by the last rays of the sun, revealing contours of the landscape unseen at earlier hours. But the title also brings up more conflicting images. Chartreuse is a yellow-green, unctuous liqueur produced by Carthusian monks residing in hermit-like seclusion in the charterhouse. The word conjures up a combination of images at once sensual and ascetic, a prefiguration of the hero's discovery of love within the confining walls of his prison.

There is a prehistory to my affair with Stendhal. Quite a while before I was entranced by his swan-song novel describing a young hero's incarceration in a fantasy Parma citadel where he falls in love with his jailer's daughter; long before I imagined accompanying Fabrice del Dongo to his elevated prison cell in the Farnese Tower, I myself had discovered aerial exaltation in my own "tower"—the tower of San Gimignano. We all called it my "tower." It was the tiny room I occupied at the top of the villa my parents had rented on the Normandy coast at the beginning of the war, shortly before the German invasion. For reasons no one ever questioned, the villa carried the name of the Italian town San Gimignano. At the time—I was all of sixteen—I knew as little about Tuscany as I did about Stendhal. But the musical sound of "San Gimignano," the lofty privacy in my retreat, reachable by a narrow staircase, and the illusion of freedom in this confined space where I penned love letters on a monastic desk (vaguely plagiarizing some Romantic poet)—all this prepared me, I believe, to become, a few years later, an awestruck reader of *The Charterhouse of Parma*.

• • •

Stendhal was born in Grenoble, only a short distance from the striking, pre-Alpine setting of the Grande Chartreuse monastery. He admired the dramatic vistas near his native city, but his favorite landscapes were those of Italy. They had for him a distinctly musical quality. As an epigraph to *The Charterhouse of Parma* he chose lines from a poem by

Ludovico Ariosto linking the poet's desire to write to the inspiration of enchanting landscapes:

> *Già mi fur dolci inviti a empir le carte*
> *I luoghi ameni*

> (Charming sites have always been for me
> Tender solicitations to put words to paper)

Stendhal's favorite *luoghi ameni* (from the classical *locus amoenus*) were, above all, in northern Italy: the hilly banks of Lake Como, the peaks of the Alps viewed from Griante, the twin branches of the lake surveyed from the princely villa Sfondrata, set above the village of Bellagio; and Lake Maggiore, with its sumptuous Borromean Islands famous for their gardens. It is precisely in the setting of Lake Como, which Stendhal evoked so often in rapturous terms, that Fabrice, his dashing young hero, is raised and has his early adventures. It is also there, in this sensuous setting, that Fabrice's passionate aunt Gina Pietranera falls in love with him.

Stendhal liked to think of landscapes in terms of musical themes and variations. His fictional writings themselves constantly respond to an inner music playing staccato effects against tender moments, irony against illusions, disenchantment against enthusiasm, negation against affirmation. It is hardly surprising that he was a devotee of Mozart's operas.

Once Henri Beyle (Stendhal's real name) was appointed consul in the forlorn papal port of Civitavecchia, he repeatedly escaped to nearby Rome, which competed in his mind with the enticements of the lake region. Two major texts record his fascination with the city of the seven hills: *Rome, Naples et Florence* (1817) and *Promenades dans Rome* (1829). Stendhal became our guide during our Fulbright year, as we set out on strolls through forums, along the banks of the Tiber, and in the more popular quarters of Trastevere. Following his footsteps, our walks took us to the old streets near the Pantheon, to Palazzo Farnese, to Campo de' Fiori, to Piazza Navona, where we never failed to pause near Bernini's fountain with its four river gods. We developed a special fondness for Via Giulia, so named after Pope Julius II, responsible for the Renaissance urbanistic renewal of the city. We strolled through historic quarters, all the while reading *Promenades dans Rome*. I had bought the three little volumes of the Divan edition in a bookstore on Piazza della Minerva, which features a sculpture of an elephant carrying an obelisk. It was assuredly the right place for the purchase of this work, for Stendhal had made it a habit to stop at a famous hotel, the former Palazzo Fonsecca, situated on that piazza.

The Rome of 1950 through which Stendhal guided us was steeped in divisive political passions. The war was not forgotten. The city was still recovering from nightmarish times. Peace had returned, but memories of the excesses of the fascist regime, of German reprisals, of postwar vendettas, were very much alive. Jeep-riding squads known as the *celere*, created by the hardfisted Minister of the Interior Mario Scelba, had been suppressing Communist rallies, as well as neofascist demonstrations. Stendhal knew, of course, all about war. As a young man, he had crossed the Alps into Italy with Napoleon Bonaparte's army (the memory of which served as the allegro overture of *The Charterhouse of Parma*), and years later he saw Moscow burn, and participated in the catastrophic winter retreat from Russia.

And he knew about stormy times and violent political changes. His major works—*The Red and the Black*, *Lucien Leuwen*, *The Charterhouse of Parma*, as well as his travel writings and cultural articles—are without exception political in their keen perception of the contemporary scene. Born in 1783, he had lived through an unusual number of crises and regime changes in rapid succession: the Revolution of 1789, the Reign of Terror in 1793, the Directory, the Consulate, the Empire, the fall of Napoleon after Waterloo, the Restoration of the Bourbons, the constitutional monarchy of 1830, and the reign of Louis Philippe. Stendhal was arguably the shrewdest diagnostician of the acceleration of history that created a rift between generations, discord between fathers and sons.

There was something, however, that affected me more than Stendhal's often provocative political assessments or the political texture of his fictional plots. It was the tone, the delightful *chaud-froid* of his style, the Mozartian counterpoint of lyricism and irony—an irony that protects rather than undercuts the tender moments. The more I read him, the more I became attached to this disabused, but never disenchanted, daydreamer. I was evidently converted to *Beylisme* (a word invented by Stendhal himself after his real name, Henri Beyle), which to his fervent admirers represents a very special outlook on life, both skeptical and enthusiastic, a lucid willingness to be taken in by one's own dreams—above all, a way at once clearheaded and amused of watching oneself live as an unpredictable *Other* in pursuit of elusive happiness.

It is hardly surprising that when, still a fledgling instructor, I was entrusted with giving a graduate seminar on Stendhal, I rushed to discuss the tremors of his style, his teasing indirections, his oblique interventions in the narrative, the shifting lines and ceaseless shuttle—so typical of his work—between lived experience and the written word. My haste in displaying insight into the inner workings of his art was no doubt characteristic of a fresh PhD's impatience to move swiftly to sophisticated complexities. I wanted to disentangle the subtle interlacings of memory and invention, and probe the secrets of Stendhal's craft in creating an elusive yet omnipresent narrator-persona.

In time, I became more moderate and open to a range of approaches. Stendhal himself, always wary of abstractions, served as a warning. As we were reading in *The Red and the Black* about ambitious Julien Sorel's career and tragic end in post-Revolutionary France, our class discussions moved toward more concrete social, psychological, and political issues: the historic circumstances, the conflicting temperaments of Madame de Rênal and Mathilde de La Mole, the bitterness of class resentments, the reactionary ideologies and policies after the fall of Napoleon, the symbol of the guillotine, the advent of the Industrial Revolution, and the new cult of money.

And there was a deeper lesson. Listening to my students' diversity of comments and interpretations I came to realize that even though our personal rapport with a writer remains essentially an intimate matter, the study of literary texts in the collective and stimulating atmosphere of a classroom discussion will at its best—and with the best of writers—lead to fresh and inventive readings. This struck me as especially evident in the case of Stendhal. His teasing pirouettes, his playful discontinuities, his narrative indirections, make of every rereading a rediscovery. "*On n'en a jamais fini avec Stendhal,*" I once heard an admirer say. So true. We're never done with Monsieur Beyle.

13 · Baudelaire: Visions of Paris

"The old Paris no longer exists," Baudelaire complains in a celebrated poem about the pariahs of this world, and about his own mournful nostalgia. The thirteen stanzas of "*Le cygne*" (The Swan) refer to the radical transformations of certain historic quarters of the capital as a result of Baron Haussmann's ambitious projects of urban renewal at the beginning of the Second Empire. Napoleon III had appointed him in 1853 to embellish the city by creating broad modern boulevards, but also for the less publicized purpose of allowing troops and artillery to prevent popular uprisings such as those of 1830 and 1848, when barricades blocked the narrow streets.

When *Les fleurs du mal* (The Flowers of Evil) appeared in 1857, entire city blocks, whole quarters, had been gutted. In memorable lines, Baudelaire laments that the face of Paris was changing more quickly than the human heart. The poet was not alone in being enamored of the picturesque asperities of the old center, the complicated charm of its irregular surfaces, even of the painful excitement of scaffolds serving to dismantle *le vieux Paris*.

Not all was loss and nostalgia. Some outlying districts like Auteuil and Passy had retained their provincial flavor. In the center of the city, sound and movement captivated the stroller. Baudelaire's flâneur is at times almost deafened by the din of the horse-drawn omnibus that took an hour to cross from the Panthéon to Courcelles. It was also the period of outsized posters or placards. Certain quarters featured specialized professions: dog clippers, basket menders, *réveilleuses*—women who for five centimes came to wake up their clients—and other women who rented out and applied leeches. Renting umbrellas was a gainful occupation in the vicinity of cemeteries. Grocers, carpenters, masons, still wore traditional costumes. The melancholic *cris de Paris* that asthmatic Marcel Proust could hear from his bedroom filled the air at certain hours—"Oison, pijon, Gatel à fève"; the rag dealer's drawn-out, immensely sad "Habits, chiffons"—and continued for years to resound in the Latin Quarter, like obsessive refrains.

Baudelaire was acutely aware of these wailing, often discordant street chants in the early morning hours, like the call of the ambulant window pane installer in the distinctly perverse prose poem "Le mauvais vitrier" (The Bad Glazier) who is called to climb all the way to the sixth floor, only to be sent down again and fall on his load of breakable window panes. Even such absurdly cruel dreams are linked to Baudelaire's weirdly poetic Parisian scene.

The poet's familiarity with Paris extends to quaint, often forlorn places associated with intimate experiences: the old Hotel d'Aligre, at the corner of the rue des Deux-Portes in the working class quarter that became the 20ème Arrondissement; the district of Cluny, the setting of his erotic devotion to his "black Venus" Jeanne Duval; the Passage of the Pont Neuf where on a certain night he found himself desperately searching for an elusive rhyme; the dubious establishment in the Latin Quarter where he probably contracted the venereal disease that led to his aphasia and death. Ironically, his intimacy with various parts of the capital was largely the result of harassment by creditors who pursued him for unpaid debts, forcing him frequently to move to distant new dwellings to avoid the fearful debtors' prison located, as he knew only too well, in a dead end near the rue de Clichy.

Pursued and humiliated, Baudelaire seemed to be forever on the escape, on a clandestine move across the big city to a new domicile, feeling safe again, as well as in exile. For a while, he lived in destitution on the rue de Seine, and would walk from the rue de Hautefeuille to the banks of the Seine. At some other time, he dwelled in an aristocratic *hôtel particulier*, a town house, on the tiny St. Louis Island—a place that lovers of historic sites continued to visit because the second floor of the Hôtel de Lauzun had for a while housed the notorious "Club des Haschichins," where the opium-consuming poet had for a while occupied a room and a study.

Baudelaire was a tireless stroller. But if he spent hours, often at night, frequenting the narrow streets or alleys as though seeking to unravel a mystery, it may well have been out of a settled distaste for his lodging. "I saw the horror of my hovel," he laments in one of his Parisian poems. Diary notes provide an unmistakable allusion to Blaise Pascal's assertion in his *Pensées* that humanity's misery comes from the unwillingness to remain monastically secluded in a room. Baudelaire even envisaged writing a study of the "great illness" of feeling horror for one's dwelling.

However intense the poet's horror of his confining rooms may have been, the walls that isolated him from the outside world represented a refuge, a respite, or at least the illusion of a respite, from his persistent sense of anguish. In the prose poem "À une heure du matin" (At 1:00 a.m.), he describes himself reaching his room, still deafened by the din of street noises, eager for silence and sleep. Darkness itself feels like a defense against the aggressive outside. He concludes tersely, condemning both life and the city: "Horrible vie! Horrible ville!" More than one piece of "Tableaux parisiens" evokes the ambiguous effort to escape from what the poet, with deliberate vagueness, defines as "le mystère" and "l'absurdité."

The oceanic megalopolis nonetheless remains appealing, even though the soul finds itself in constant peril of drowning. The flow of crowds allows for a protective anonymity. Losing oneself in the mass has for Baudelaire a poetic, even a philosophical, potential. Poetic, because this immersion carries one along by a current stronger than oneself, thus allowing one to surrender to the magic of the unpredictable. Philosophical, because the crowd can make one love the sense of *self* in a communion that the poet provokingly defines as a "sainte prostitution de l'âme" (a holy prostitution of the soul). The prose poem "Les foules" (The Crowds) suggests that it is not given to everyone to experience such an immersion in the multitude, that the art of melting into a crowd offers the rare privilege of being all at once a *self* and *others*. "I go to bed," we read in another prose poem, "taking pride in having lived and suffered in others." But this pride comes less from love for humanity than from a need for inebriation and a taste for dissolution in every sense of that word.

Baudelaire's perfect flâneur cultivates the art of circulating in Paris incognito. He is a dreamer about non-being and about the unknown, insatiably attracted to the "*non-moi*," to what is not himself. This strolling flâneur, carried along by the flow of the street crowds, knows full well from his readings that the arteries of the city carry an intense poetic charge. He admired Balzac for his transfigurative vision of the vast plateau lying between the heights of Montmartre and Montrouge—a valley filled with suffering and tears, false joys, and monstrosities. It was a valley that the incomparable novelist metaphorized into a fathomless ocean hiding mysterious treasures at its unreachable bottom.

The very pages of "The Heroism of Modern Life" that contain Baudelaire's ecstatic praise of Balzac also extol the poetic fecundity of Paris for an attentive observer: "The supernatural surrounds and sustains us" ("Le merveilleux nous enveloppe et nous abreuve"). Modernity, a loaded word in the poet's essays, most often refers to a peculiar contemporary sense of beauty, both artful and discordant. Even the gloomy masculine outer garment, dark symbol of perpetual mourning, provides unaccountable thrills. The streets of Paris, undergoing the brutal haussmannian transformations, offer nevertheless a sense of wounding beauty. "The deafening street roared all around me" ("La rue assourdissante autour de moi hurlait")—that is the first line of one of the *Tableaux parisiens*. But the aggressive uproar of the streets, their incessant movement, even chaos, also offer tonic satisfactions to the senses. Though jarred by the din and the confusion, Baudelaire transmutes the street into a "river of vitality" and the circulating crowd into an immense reservoir of electricity.

A poem dedicated to Victor Hugo refers to Paris as the city where unsuspected mysteries spread through its organs like nourishing saps. Even horror may cast its spell in the form of decrepit, disjointed human shapes. "Les sept vieillards" (The Seven Old Men) begins with lines that T.S. Eliot well remembered as he wrote *The Waste Land*:

> Fourmillante cité, cité pleine de rêves,
> Où le spectre en plein jour raccroche le passant
>
> (Teeming city, city filled with dreams,
> Where a specter can take hold of the stroller in full daylight).

In the peripheral old streets of the faubourg, one may come across a sickly, pale girl with red hair—a *mendiante rousse*, a young beggar dressed in rags, whom the poet's imagination transforms into a regal silhouette worthy of appearing in a glamorous work of fiction.

Even better, in his daydreaming walks, the poet may stumble on a rare metaphor, an inspired alliance of words, a precious rhyme. In stunning lines, Baudelaire evokes in "Le soleil" the thrills of such street revelations, tripping ("trébuche") as though over paving stones. Most frequently, however, Baudelaire's Paris is not sunny, but drizzly, foggy, rheumatic. It may well be that true lovers of Paris love it best when its sidewalks are wet and shiny, and everything—roofs, trees, passersby, the sky itself—blends in a universal grayness. Humidity pervades *Les fleurs du mal*. "Brumes et pluies" (Fog and Rain) is the title of one of the funereal poems of the collection, evoking vaporous shrouds and gloomy darkness. The "Spleen" poems are especially loaded with images of long rainy days. In one of them, the poet compares himself to a "king of a rainy land." Another famously begins with the ambiguous word "Pluviôse," which refers to the rainy period of late January and February, and was chosen to designate the fifth month of the French Revolutionary calendar. It also suggests the chilly flood of gloom affecting the city's inhabitants, reminding them of their mortality.

As though fog and rain did not suffice to veil the mysteries Baudelaire suspects lie hidden in the dark corners of the capital, many of his most effective descriptions are set during the crepuscular hours, those multi-layered hours of dusk when, as he put it, "the sky's curtains close." These are the fleeting moments of evening's tender and imprecise colors, leading to the night, and to the sick and the dying. "Crépuscule du soir" (Dusk) evokes indeed the sighs and moans echoing through hospitals in the middle of the night, when suffering becomes more acute. Baudelaire seems haunted by the image of the hospital. Suffering from insomnia, he thinks of the terminally ill. Images of hospital rooms come up in unexpected contexts. The work of Rembrandt is likened in "Les phares" to a "sad hospital filled with murmurs." Life itself is compared to a hospital where every patient is possessed by the desire to move to another bed. Illness and death even become protagonists. Already in *La fanfarlo*, an early novella published when he was in his twenties, he imagines Mortality joyously invading hospitals. Twenty years later, hospitals still appear in the epilogue to the prose poems—only this time they are explicitly juxtaposed to bordellos, to purgatory, even to Hell. In many ways, this epilogue to the prose poems gathered in "Le Spleen de

Paris" provides a key to the poet's vision of the city. Suffering and vice, illness and love, death and eros appear as inseparable couples to one who knew full well that he owed his physical degradation to his venereal pursuits and, more precisely, to the *Treponema pallidum* of syphilis.

"I love you, oh infamous capital!" This outcry in the epilogue follows right after the metaphor of the whorish city, the *énorme catin*, whose "infernal charm" continues to spellbind the poet. In *The Painter of Modern Life*, a series of incisive essays, he describes with some crudeness the *foemina simplex* of Juvenal's Roman satire, a female type that was still to be found among the sex slaves of the modern city—heavy, dull, sprawled women displaying their flesh on sofas, their eyes glazed by addiction to spirits. These macabre nymphs embody for Baudelaire the "infamous" essence of the capital's alluring vice and hellish enticements. His own eyes are wide open (his nostrils are more delicate) when it comes to sordid urban aspects. He stares at the dirty water running along the sidewalks, carrying its secrets to the sewer. Crime and sin ooze from the walls, as they also ooze from the daily newspapers. The poet is struck by street visions of sin *incarnate*. The seven crippled old men of the already mentioned poem, dressed in yellow rags, with their mean glance, their sword-like beards reminding him of Judas, and their decrepit walk as though treading on corpses, become the living metaphors of the seven deadly sins.

"Au lecteur," the preliminary poem of *Les fleurs du mal*, treats the reader as a hypocritical accomplice and claims that Satan pulls all the strings, having us take delight in repugnant things, daily pushing us further downward toward Hell. But long before reaching the bottom, perhaps because of an overdose of sordid images, Baudelaire becomes entranced by his own nightmarish vision and gives in to overwhelming compassion. He watches decrepit widows, monstrously dislocated, who have long ago ceased being attractive and who now walk like wounded animals. Yet Baudelaire does not recoil in disgust. Instead, he has us share his feelings of pity. Hunchbacked and all twisted, these old women are still to be loved: "Let us love them! They still are souls" ("aimons-les! Ce sont encore des âmes.").

The imploring eyes of the poor and the beggars unsettle him especially. In one of his prose poems, Baudelaire asserts that the mute eloquence and reproachful humility of these expressive eyes must unfailingly move any sensitive person deeply.

•   •   •

But how does this compassion fit into the broader context of Baudelaire's often haughty aesthetic and moral views? His vision of the transformed and transforming capital is manifestly linked to a provocative conception of modern beauty. Paris means jarring change and movement—the very opposite of a fixed reality subject to immutable laws. Baudelaire never deviated from a belief in the ephemeral nature of beauty. "Absolute, eternal beauty does not exist," he pontificated in one of his articles of art criticism. The "Salon de 1846," in certain passages, attempts to compete with Stendhal's provocative impertinences on the subject of aesthetic relativism. Baudelaire's pleasure in movement, his taste for the fugacious and the evanescent, might explain his readiness to celebrate the transitory character of the city, even some motions of the abhorred natural world, such as the movement of the "marvelous clouds" in transit ("J'aime les nuages . . . les nuages qui passent . . . là-bas . . . les meveilleux nuages.").

Attraction to the bizarre and the outright ugly proves to be central to the poet's vision of Paris. In notes scribbled to himself, he sets as a goal finding strange and horrible city adventures. This search for the repulsive and the outlandish is not a fleeting caprice. It takes on the features of a major motif, that of the fecundity of ugliness, announced early in a preliminary poem of the collection: "We find attraction in repugnant things." And if the angel in "L'irrémédiable," tempted by love of the deformed, struggles in the miasma and among the slimy monsters of a nightmare, this is surely because for the poet as well "that which is not slightly deformed seems insensitive." The true lover of beauty, accordingly, savors above all the most unexpected dissonances as exquisite nutrition for the soul.

Baudelaire is moreover convinced that art signifies artifice, that beauty always exists and shines as a creation of the human mind. Resolutely not a devotee of rural nature, he indulged neither in the seductions of countryside chlorophyll nor in the innocent warble of birds. Reluctant to compete with some of his predecessors who sang of consoling forests and placid lakes as idealized settings for noble emotions, he rather thought of beauty as a *rêve de pierre* (a dream of stone) and of cities as "stone landscapes caressed by fog."

This distaste for Mother Nature—hostility might be a more suitable term—finds its way onto many pages. At times, it shows up with reference to the "hideousness of fecundity," or to the "frigid majesty of the sterile woman." Eros may be significant in the poet's work, but it never functions in the service of procreation. Pregnancy makes its appearance as a *"maladie d'araignée,"* a spider's illness. As for his notable aversion to vegetation, it casts some light on the praise of "mineral" landscapes he so lavishly expresses in a prose poem carrying the slightly ungrammatical English title "Any Where Out of the World," which describes a dream city:

> This city is near a body of water. They say it is built of marble, and that people there have such hatred of the vegetal that they uproot all the trees. Now there is a landscape according to your taste, a landscape made of light and mineral, and water to reflect them.

In an erotic vein, Samuel Cramer, the young poet in *La Fanfarlo*, watching his mistress undress in a most natural manner under the circumstances, orders her to get dressed again immediately, and to appear to him in her theatrical costume and makeup. "I want Colombine," (that was her theatrical role), "give me Colombine again; give her to me as she appeared the night she drove me wild with her odd vestment and circus bodice." No wonder Samuel Cramer likes all glittering objects and would gladly repaint all the trees and even the sky. Above all, it is not surprising that Baudelaire has written an essay in praise of makeup, "Éloge du maquillage."

The proclaimed hostility to vegetation and to nature in general, the preference for artifice and "the dream of stone," almost take on metaphysical dimensions. Disdainful of the optimistic pantheism of some of his literary predecessors, who tended to spiritualize nature, Baudelaire stuck to his conviction that both beauty and morality were strictly human creations. At every turn, he took a position contrary to that of a Jean-Jacques Rousseau. It is evil, according to his view, not good, that comes "naturally."

Can one speak, as some like to do, of Baudelaire's *surrealism*, or superrealism? The fairy-tale poem "Rêve parisien" (Parisian Dream), among others, would support such an opinion, filled as it is with dazzling images of a "terrible landscape" appearing to him in a dream "full of miracles," and in the midst of the "inebriating monotony" of metal, marble, and water. The poem is studded with oneiric imagery: a "Babel of stairways and arcades," an unusual setting of "heavy cataracts," of crystal curtains, walls of metal, cascades of gold, urns from which diamonds keep pouring, tunnels of gems that lead to an "eternity of silence."

This surrealism avant la lettre characterizes also the modernity of Baudelaire—a modernity especially striking in "Le cygne" (The Swan), where the poet resorts to modern poetry's favorite device of juxtaposing the mythical and the familiar, as well as conflating the present and the distant past. This justly celebrated poem describes how the poet, crossing the new Carrousel in chaotic transformation, notices a swan that apparently escaped from its cage in a menagerie. The animal is desperately seeking some water on the dry Parisian soil. This swan becomes for Baudelaire a symbol of exile. Without any transition or explanation, the poet brings up Andromache, the widow of Hector, killed by Achilles at Troy. She also is an exile, living out her homeless existence in faithful remembrance.

The rich resonances of "The Swan" depend in large measure on its complex and evocative inner music, but even more so on a context that includes, in addition to the thirsty swan and to bereft Andromache, a tubercular Black woman lost in the arid urban landscape, vainly searching for the absent coconut trees of her native Africa.

The dehydrated swan, the phthisic African woman, Andromache mourning her dead husband, are all symbolic incarnations of loss and alienation. In Baudelaire's visionary poem, Paris appears as the city of exile and ecstatic recollection. With its unexpected dissonances, it shares some features with what will soon become familiar to readers of Franz Kafka's Prague, James Joyce's Dublin, and Alfred Döblin's hectic Berlin—cities of the mind, where humans live in a state of estrangement.

But Baudelaire considers it a privileged, even elating estrangement. In one of his self-revelatory texts, the prose poem "Les foules" (The Crowds), the proud flâneur, delighted to immerse himself in the multitude (a talent not given to everyone), experiences a vision of Paris that turns into a vision of his own discordant self. Yet the elating estrangement of his immersions in the multitude ("bain de multitude" is the bold metaphor) allows him to bask in the inebriation of a valued solitude. Other texts echo this special delight in circulating incognito, inside a crowd, amid the rubble and upheaval of haussmannian transformations of le vieux Paris.

This vision of urban crowds and cityscapes is ultimately self-directed, asserting pride in the integrity of the self in its contact with the multitude. The poet's *promeneur solitaire*, altogether different from the one made famous by Rousseau, undergoes a powerful intoxication that allows him, when in physical contact with the multitude, to remain all at once himself, as well as in indiscriminate communion with all the others.

14 · The Year of the Eiffel Tower

1889 was the year when France commemorated the centennial of the Revolution. In that year, the apotheosis of Victor Hugo, high priest of democratic virtues, whose remains an entire population had accompanied to the Pantheon, was still a fresh memory. Hugo's life (1802–1885) and work almost literally filled the century, and it was the century he had come to embody that was now being celebrated.

The festive commemoration of the fall of the Bastille was meant to glorify the nineteenth century as an age of progress. It was a century that began under the shadow of the Revolution, and that repeatedly revived revolutionary dreams and fervor. It had, however, also turned out to be a century of discontinuities, counterrevolutions, and repression. The year of Waterloo, 1815, can be viewed as pivotal, an end of a regime, but also a new beginning—and so were 1830, 1848, and 1870, all of them dramatic dates that marked a forward thrust as well as a regression and relapse into the past. But in 1889, the Third Republic, the regime in power, could claim that it was the undisputed heir to the principles of 1789.

The Eiffel Tower, the outstanding monument of the Exposition Universelle, was 1889's answer to the razed Bastille. Its erection monumentalized the achievements of the century, even though some ironically inclined minds complained about its gigantic funnel-shaped form and the architect's obscene delusions of grandeur. For most, however, the three-hundred-meter-high steel architecture became the appropriate symbol of the historic occasion. In that year of the Exposition Universelle, there was an all-pervasive display of the outsized: allegorical ceremonies, immense exhibits, dazzling illuminations, solemn inaugurations (the great amphitheater of the Sorbonne, among others), massive parades. On August 18, more than fifteen thousand mayors of metropolitan France and overseas territories paraded in ceremonial garb. The centennial also consecrated the preeminence of Paris, capital and heart of the nation. More than that: it was glorifying Paris, in Walter Benjamin's famous phrasing, as the capital of the nineteenth century.

Neither Paris, nor France, were single-voiced in their appraisal of the republican mystique. During the last three decades of the nineteenth century, the principles of the Third Republic (which lasted until the French defeat of 1940) rested on the ideological pillars of anticlerical *laïcité* (or secularism), combative optimism, financial opportunism, parliamentary factions, and chauvinistic patriotic poses. This complex republican ideology, however, did not go unchallenged. Frontal attacks on the scientific spirit, as well as on the *intellectuels* in general, coincided with the euphoric celebrations of the centennial. These attacks were not new. As early as the 1840s, various pamphlets and books, largely encouraged by a sectarian Catholic press, had denounced the pernicious influence of professors on France's youth. The last two decades of the nineteenth century witnessed a major offensive against the intellectual establishment. Paul Bourget's central thesis in his widely read novel, *Le disciple*, which appeared in 1889—the very year of the Eiffel Tower—was that teachers, associated with the central tenets of scientism and democracy, should be held directly responsible for the moral effects of their dangerous philosophy on their students.

In the wake of the humiliating defeat of the Franco-Prussian war of 1870, followed by the trauma of the Commune, Bourget and his followers sought salvation in traditionalism and intransigent nationalism, denouncing intellectuals as subverters of conservative values. Many of the anti-intellectual pronouncements of the late 1880s, and beyond, condemned the academic elites as a new class of mandarins who considered themselves the spiritual guides of a democracy that came to be known as "la république des professeurs"—academics who, with their ideological teachings, had corrupted an impressionable younger generation, thus undermining France's finest traditions. The real target of these attacks was of course the democratic mystique itself and, beyond that, the tenets of the Revolution held responsible for all the contemporary social and moral ills.

But critical assessments of the legacy of the Revolution also found their way into the writings of the decried intellectual masters. Hippolyte Taine's *Les origines de la France contemporaine* (1875–93) was hostile to the revolutionary leaders, naming Danton a "political butcher" and Robespierre "the ultimate runt." Even Ernest Renan, though he considered the Revolution the "sublime" French epic, in the final analysis came to judge it a failure ("une expérience manquée"), and even an "odious and horrible" event that in its consequences bureaucratized France, leaving it a spiritual desert where only material prosperity is valued.

The commemorative festivities of 1889 were hardly necessary to remind the French of their revolutionary past and its consequences. Many surely preferred to forget the most violent features, but these could not possibly be forgotten. Nor could the Revolution be considered a closed chapter. Its mission or ideals had never really been fulfilled. The history of the nineteenth century had been afflicted by a series of dramatic caesuras, discontinuities, and relapses: 1815, 1830, 1848, 1851, 1870. Repeated revolutionary episodes had kept the Revolution's momentum (as well as the fear of that momentum) alive: 1830, which installed the constitutional monarchy; 1848, which soon led to the coup d'état of Louis Bonaparte; the Paris Commune of 1871, which brought about a fierce repression.

It is hardly surprising that writers of literary works, from Balzac to Zola, when not dealing directly with the events of the Revolution, offer repeated allusions and references to them. Old Goriot, the central character of Balzac's famous novel, is not merely a doting and profaned father, a latter-day degraded Lear or "Christ of paternity," but, as the reader learns, he had been chairman of a revolutionary section, as well as a ruthless profiteer. During the great famine he sold wheat at black market prices to the "coupeurs de tête" (head choppers) of the sanguinary Comité de Salut Public. Danton and Robespierre are repeatedly mentioned with awe, fear, and respect in Stendhal's *The Red and the Black* (1831), whose leading epigraph quotes a stark statement about the bitter truth attributed to Danton: "La vérité, l'âpre vérité." The reader is given to understand that Julien Sorel's plebeian anger is fraught with a revolutionary potential. As for *Germinal* (1885), Zola's novel about a coalminers' strike published shortly before the year of the Eiffel Tower, its title is the name of the month marking the beginning of spring in the

French Republican calendar instituted by the Convention in the grim year 1793, the year of the Terror. Yet the word "Germinal" also signals the novel's hope-filled theme of the moral and political awakening of the working class, implying necessary struggles lying ahead. Zola's ambivalent title thus points in opposing directions. "Germinal" marks a renewal, the germination of life, a thrust toward the future. It also connotes an anachronistic calendar of the past, associated with violence and destruction.

A bidirectional perspective characterizes the French collective consciousness in the post-revolutionary period. The nineteenth century seemed determined (or condemned) to think forward by looking backward. The future and the past came into ironic tension, not merely because of repeated attempts at "restoration," at setting the clock back and treating the events ranging from 1789 to the fall of Napoleon in 1815 as a scandalous parenthesis, but because progress-oriented ideologues seemed compelled repeatedly to look to already anachronistic models for inspiration. French history during the entire century thus appears both linear and repetitive. Commenting on the turbulent events of 1848–51 that led to the imperial regime of Napoleon III, Karl Marx famously observed that historical events and personages tend to repeat themselves, the first time as tragedy, and later as farce. This deflating observation was strikingly illustrated by Gustave Flaubert in the chapter on political clubs in *L'Éducation sentimentale*—a truly hilarious episode of the novel, describing the orgy of rhetoric and bad faith, the farcical imitations of past public figures like Marat or Danton, while the presiding officer tries to resemble Blanqui, who in his turn tries to copy Robespierre.

Flaubert was hostile to political activism, and basically fearful of popular uprisings. His lifelong escape into aestheticism was in part an escape from the sound and fury of history in the making. Other contemporaries, however, as they witnessed the acceleration of events, welcomed becoming and change, and justified the deeper meanings of revolutions. While deploring the crimes committed, these apologists saw the drama of the French Revolution as part of a divine scenario, as the will of a God who knows no rest, whose work remains forever unfinished. God as revolutionary! The writings of many Romantics— Victor Hugo's *Les Misérables*, as well as his *La Légende de siècles* are prime examples—illustrate the notion that a supreme spiritual force energizes history and the evolution of humanity toward its ideal destiny.

It is, however, a new kind of history: the history of the human soul. *La Légende des siècles* was to be articulated on the epic adventure of humankind throughout the ages: the mythical world of gods and monsters, Biblical times, the civilizations of Greece and Rome, the Christian ages, the Renaissance, the contemporary setting, the as yet uncharted future. But the French Revolution was to be the central panel of this ambitious poem.

Despite a general reluctance to dwell on some of the revolting aspects of the revolutionary events (especially the Terror and the reign of the guillotine), an impressive number of important histories of the Revolution were published throughout the nineteenth century. The most compelling of them, in large part because of its mythopoetic qualities and lyrical flights, is Jules Michelet's *Histoire de la Révolution française*, written between 1843 and 1853, during one of the most turbulent periods of popular uprisings and violent regime changes. The book was consecrated by a national edition in the celebratory year 1889—the year of the Eiffel Tower.

It would seem that the commemorative spirit was embedded in the revolutionary period itself, which proved to be exceedingly date-conscious: July 14 (the fall of the Bastille); October 6 (the march on Versailles); June 20 (the oath of the deputies in the Jeu de Paume); August 10 (the storming of the Tuileries)—not to mention September 21 (the proclamation of the Republic); Germinal (the bread riots); Thermidor (the fall of Robespierre). All these dates, as well as the names of months in the new Republican calendar, quickly became household references. Retrospectively, however, the entire revolutionary epoch remains politically and thematically polarized between two symbolic dates: 1789 and 1793, the year of the storming of the Bastille, and the year of the Terror. These two dates remain engraved in France's collective consciousness. They continue to represent two conflicting perspectives on the Revolution.

1789 heralds the myth of the Bastille, symbol of the ancien régime. Its storming by a popular uprising is perceived both as a closing and inaugural moment, a liberating event celebrated immediately in countless tracts, pamphlets, dramatic dialogues, and poems. Two centuries later, July 14 continued to be associated with a collective euphoria. It is a joyful date, as attested by the music and dancing that have become traditional every year in the streets of all French towns.

1793 is the other key date of the Revolution. Its symbolic significance, however, is far from festive. The ominous silhouette of the guillotine during that somber year fascinated Victor Hugo, in sharp contrast to Michelet's dithyrambic attachment to 1789. In his last novel, *Quatrevingt-treize* (Ninety-Three), written shortly after the violent events of the Commune, Hugo describes the grim year of the Terror as a theater of cruelty. Inflexible doctrinaires and demagogues led France to an apocalypse. Violence escalated into savagery. No mercy ("Pas de quartier") seems to have been the watchword. Yet the catastrophic nature of that bloody year 1793 also endowed it with an epic dimension appealing to the oneiric imagination of Hugo who, referring to the excesses of that *année terrible*, resorts repeatedly to metaphors of storms, shipwrecks, and the horrors of the abyss.

Larger forces were felt to be at work—and not just by Hugo—forces far more powerful than the flawed political protagonists who destroy one another; more forceful even than the mobs that storm fortresses and sack royal residences. A lingering awe, as well as malaise, was felt by many in France about the Revolution, which ultimately came to be symbolized by the scaffold, the guillotine, and the dreaded figure of the Executioner.

The euphoric ceremonial celebrations of 1889, the year of the Eiffel Tower, signaled a determined generalized effort to erase these troubling images by focusing on the initial moment, the assault on the Bastille. The efforts to forget, the attempts to efface or repress the ultimate revolutionary episode—the regicidal event of January 21, 1793—were not, however, altogether successful. The beheading of the King was vaguely but disturbingly perceived as a parricide, even a deicide. Internal political strife remained very much alive behind the festive façade of the commemorative Exposition Universelle of 1889. Behind its seeming stability and prosperity, the long-lived Third Republic (1870–1940), which came to an end with World War II, proved in reality to be a period of exacerbated political and social tensions, bordering at times on ideological and even physical violence.

Not long after the Eiffel Tower was erected as a symbol of modern civilization and human progress, the infamous Dreyfus case was to tear apart the fabric of French social and intellectual life. Vile anti-Semitism was only part of a more generalized syndrome of nationalism, chauvinism, epidemic bigotry—and, for significant segments of the population, discomfort with the heritage of the Revolution. To be sure, the moral principles and democratic ideals of that heritage were also fervently defended. The self-congratulatory year of 1889 voiced, in contrapuntal manner, belief in progress and nostalgia for a lost order, at times viewing God and his designs in the service of melioristic concepts, at others challenging the notion of progress and of forward-looking history.

1889—the year of *panthéonisations*, triumphal odes, triumphal statues, carton-pâte historical reconstitutions, and the erection and inauguration of the three-hundred-meter-high tower, is not merely the year of self-adulating, pompous festivities. The commemoration of the Revolution was articulated on two conflicting dates (and realities): one inaugural (1789), the other catastrophic (1793). What they do have in common is that together they set up the model of events at the same time exceptional and radically destructive, thus raising the curtain on what was to become in France an era that, in constantly shifting ways, pitted political smugness against a sense of impending disaster. The German invasion of 1940 put an end to this self-satisfied and divided Third Republic.

15 · Malraux and the World of Violence

I was clearly mistaken when, on several occasions, I expected my students to respond positively to the interplay of abstract thought and revolutionary action in the work of André Malraux. It seemed evident to me that *La condition humaine* (1933) would engage them, if only because of the intellectual's provocative relation to the subject of revolution, that they would react strongly and in a very personal way according to whether they felt sympathetic or hostile to the idea of political revolution. At the very least, I counted on their interest in Malraux's fictional handling of violent action and his personal involvement in dramatic events of the twentieth century.

For Malraux was literally present at the crossroads of history in the making: in the Far East, when the wind of revolution began to blow; in the anti-fascist rallies in Europe; in the Spanish Civil War, where he organized and led an air squadron against General Franco's troops; in the French army in 1940, when he was made prisoner; in the Resistance movement, when he was captured and came close to being tortured; as a Colonel in the Free French Forces liberating Alsace; then as Minister for Information and Minister for Cultural Affairs under Charles de Gaulle— and all the while pursuing interests in archaeology, cultural history, and his death-obsessed fictional writings.

In discussing Malraux, one must beware of two traps. The one is to view him as a superior adventurer, a would-be French T. E. Lawrence (he in fact planned to write a study about him). That Malraux exhibited a strong adventurous streak is borne out by his early involvement in Indochina, and his appropriation of some Khmer statuary, which got him into serious trouble with authorities and for a while landed him in jail. But his opportunism—whether self-serving, political, or heroic—would not account for the obsessive nature of his thoughts returning again and again to the mysterious question of human destiny as we face our mortal condition.

The other trap leads to reducing all of Malraux's texts to ideological commitments, and specifically to endorsements of revolutionary action. But such a view, as I pointed out to my class, fails to account for his allegiance to de Gaulle, and even less for his notion of the "sacred" nature of art (*sacré* is a favorite word of his)—sacred not because of religious belief but because art confronts ultimate meanings and, in one way or another, deals with the human anxiety about death.

The early signals of *La condition humaine* are telling. A murder is about to be committed in a Shanghai hotel room. But Tchen, the assassin, forgets the practical revolutionary purpose of his stabbing the sleeper (to steal a document needed to obtain the weapons in the port). Instead, overwhelming anguish is all he is aware of. The word *angoisse* appears in the second sentence of the novel, reappears two paragraphs later, and again in the following pages. That semidark hotel room separated by window bars from the outside world, the world of human activities, introduces from the outset the prison imagery that will dominate later in the novel. This nocturnal world of wan light and shadows locks Tchen up in a solemn aloneness (the adjective *solennelle* appears in the opening pages). Tchen discovers himself as a *sacrificateur* rather than a fighter for a political cause.

The murder scene takes on a ceremonial character, with unmistakable suggestions of initiation and communion. Between the assassin and his victim runs a strange current. Not only is the blade, as Malraux writes, sensitive to its very tip, but a sensation of unbearable anguish passes from the struck body to Tchen's convulsive heart. Before striking the sleeping body, Tchen moreover directs the dagger against himself, stabbing himself in the arm. My class was puzzled by this clearly symbolic act, at odds, they felt, with the political purpose of the murder. Was it an early prefiguration of his own suicidal death in an act of futile terrorism? Was it a blood pact with the victim? I proposed that the opening pages of the novel determined not one, but several major themes. Death and solitude remain inescapably coupled. The moment Tchen enters the room of the murder, he also penetrates into a world of utter aloneness. Even the traffic noises seem to come from another world. As he begins to tremble, the narrative voice explains: that it was not owing to fear but because "he was alone with death," alone in a place without human beings. The alley cat that suddenly appears seems like an obscene intrusion into an otherworldly space of silence and intoxication.

During the exchange of opinions around our seminar table about Malraux's designs, I realized that even his narrative techniques can be misinterpreted. The brusque changes of scene, the staccato allure of pages reading like newspaper dispatches, seem designed to maintain suspense in a climate of revolutionary actions. The novel propels the reader swiftly from the hotel room where Tchen stabs a sleeping figure, to a nightclub where a buffoonish character drinks with prostitutes, to the street, to the port where the weapons are to be taken from a boat, to another hotel room where a woman and a man are engaged in an erotic encounter, to a shop where a child cries in pain, to a police station, to Communist headquarters, to prisoners awaiting their execution in a schoolyard. *La condition humaine* imposes a succession of shots taken from many angles. Fadeouts, close-ups, ellipses, further suggest a cinematic pace and vision. Malraux, who wrote interestingly about film techniques (see his "Esquisse d'une psychologie du cinéma"), concluded on a number of occasions that all art rested on a system of ellipses. Baroque art, he felt, could be considered a distant ancestor of the cinema because it resorted to a succession of images that prefigured the technique of découpage.

But these techniques, meant to convey the pulse of action, can also turn out to be deceptive. On closer inspection, a meditative mood prevails in the tensest moments. Dialogues and dialectic exchanges are often carried on with action as mere background noise. Not infrequently, it is difficult to remember who thought or said what, for Malraux's protagonists are in the habit of quoting one another; they appear as though contaminated by each other's meditation. And if his writings bring up, on so many pages, a climate of violence, it is not specifically the violence of revolutionary action, but a much broader violence that Malraux likens to an apocalypse. Explosions, sirens, rattling machine guns, the cries of the wounded, are all part of what Malraux calls a *fin du monde* atmosphere, or even the night of a final judgment. In *L'Espoir* (*Man's Hope*), his novel about the Spanish Civil War, an entire section is entitled "The Exercise of the Apocalypse." The congregated intellectuals, who do not cease their abstract chatter while bombs explode nearby and Madrid is aflame, are keenly aware of the self-destructive urges of Western civilization.

It was thus hardly reasonable, for a variety of reasons, to misread *La condition humaine* as a defense of the Communist revolution and its ideological propaganda, which is precisely what my students were tempted to do, while at the same time resenting such a message. We finally agreed about the one episode that most convincingly invalidates a simplistic revolutionary interpretation: Kyo's visit to the Party's official in Hankou to make clear to him that the communist sections in Shanghai should not surrender their arms, as required by Chiang Kai-shek. This episode alone would explain why the Communist Party took a rather dim view of Malraux's fictional account when it appeared. For Hankou, the one important Communist city at this point, is a dead city: no ships in the port, nothing but junks and torpedo boats; the international banks shut down, the factories deserted; the city looks like the metropolis of the unemployed. As for the Party official, he is hardly an inspiring sight: his plump body ensconced in an armchair, Vologuin's expressionless face makes him look like a somnambulist. His short, rounded back seems to belong to a hunchback. His unctuous manner of speaking comes across as another negative signal. Above all, he sees history in terms of ineluctable determinism. His repeated argument rests on blind obedience to the Party. The weapons have to be surrendered. Far from glorifying the Party, it would seem that Malraux writes about how the Party betrays its own men.

In view of the potential misreadings of *La condition humaine*, I felt that I needed to provide some information my students could not be expected to possess. The very title of the novel is a reminder of a philosophical dialogue across time between a writer of the sixteenth and a writer of the seventeenth century—a dialogue now joined by a writer of the twentieth century. For the title chosen by Malraux is an unmistakable reference to the *Essays* of Michel de Montaigne, who justified his endless indulgence in writing about his own person and behavior by asserting that every human being embodies the entire "human condition," valuing life precisely because of the ineluctable awareness of mortality. Blaise Pascal, an attentive reader of Montaigne a century later, came up with a more dramatic image of the human condition, an image directly relevant to the most somber episode in Malraux's novel, the grim pages describing the assembled political prisoners awaiting death in the schoolyard. I read Pascal's stark *pensée* about the human condition aloud to the class:

> Imagine a number of men in chains and all condemned to death; some of them each day are slaughtered in full view of the others; those who remain recognize their own condition in that of their fellow men and, looking at each other with pain, and without hope, wait for their turn. This is the image of the human condition. ("C'est l'image de la condition humaine")

I could tell that this Pascal quote had made an impression on the students. They quickly understood the obvious parallel to the dramatic scene in Malraux's novel describing the assembly of insurrectionist prisoners who are to be executed—all of them staring into the unmasked face of their common destiny. As Kyo and Katov lie side by side in the space reserved for those who are to be burned alive, they feel tied to each other by that absolute friendship without reticence which, according to Malraux, the presence of death alone can give. They live their most intense moments of communion. But it is a communion that does not depend on language. The bleeding body speaks what words cannot utter. At the tensest moment in the schoolyard scene, when the merciful poison that is to save them from the horror of the fire is dropped to the ground, it is the encounter of hands, not the voice, that offers the consolation and the love: hands brushing against each other, taking hold of each other, clutching each other in a desperate fraternity. The schoolyard scene, with its Pascalian undertones, provides an answer to the anxiety of the opening hotel room scene where solitude and death appeared as the very foundations of human existence.

Malraux's meditation on the human condition, on the mystery of "absolute friendship" and communion in the face of suffering and death, ultimately discredits the militant mode of political ideology and revolutionary action. I referred in class to a key passage in a lesser-known work of fiction carrying a Biblical title, *La lutte avec l'ange* (*The Struggle with the Angel*), part of a larger manuscript confiscated by the Gestapo, in which Malraux describes at some length a symposium of anthropologists and ethnographers gathered to discuss the permanence of the concept of humanity, and raising the central question of whether humankind is possessed with a unique destiny.

The answer does not come from the assembled intellectuals who engage in vain rhetoric. It comes, once again, in a stunning war episode, from an experience of violence. On the Eastern Front, during World War I, the German high command decided to experiment with a new chemical weapon. When the gas is released, the German soldiers move forward, across the scorched, lunar landscape, across the black grass and the dead wood, and penetrate into the enemy trenches, by now rendered defenseless. But to the astonishment of the field officers watching from afar, the soldiers fail to advance to the second line of trenches. Instead, they return, each one of them carrying a gasping, choking, fatally injured enemy. The horror has been too much for these men to bear. A human being is not made to be disintegrated in this way, nor to watch it happen, without a profound sense of rebellion. The assault wave in this allegoric passage is transformed into an assault of compassion. Something fundamental in humanity remains indestructible.

It is revealing that old Gisors, the mentor of an entire generation of revolutionaries, turns out to suffer from a paralyzed intellect, feeling unable to participate in revolutionary action. He prefers the music of serenity and the consolations of art and smoking opium. He knows that the essence of human beings is anguish and that, in his tragic isolation, despite his intelligence, he cannot penetrate into another's mind. And so, just as some escape into the wild regions of terrorism, old Gisors seeks refuge in the realm of art and opium, from where he can contemplate his solitude.

Even more telling is the presence in the novel of Kama, the painter, for whom art is an almost religious experience. He communicates typically through a disciple-interpreter. Literally and figuratively, Kama speaks another language. His voice comes from elsewhere. There seems to be a special meaning to the epilogue of *La condition humaine*, which takes place in Kama's house, where old Gisors seeks a refuge for meditation to the accompaniment of serene music. The full meaning of Kama's spiritual message reveals art as a mystical acceptance of the world, a communion with all there is, a harmony capable of overcoming solitude and even death. Malraux himself, in any number of nonfictional texts, maintained that art alone can defeat both death and solitude. The meaning of art is for him bound to its struggle with meaning, and it is this struggle that deserves the word *sacré*.

"Tout art sacré s'oppose à la mort" (All sacred art stands against death). Malraux's formula could not be clearer. Every civilization, he repeated in several texts, is haunted by what and how it thinks about mortality, by the meaning it bestows on suffering and death. That essentially defines the underlying subject of his "imaginary museum," which is the title of one of his books on art. If masterpieces are said to be immortal, this is not only because they live in an "ungraspable time" (an *insaisissable temps*), as he puts it in pages on Pablo Picasso, but because they read into every gesture and pose the mystery of suffering and the grandeur of human awareness of mortality. This awareness transcends political and cultural differences.

The attempt to feature the notion of the "sacred" casts light on Malraux's repeated temptation to produce very unorthodox texts of art history, resorting to the fiction of an imaginary museum that would juxtapose artifacts from different ages and radically different civilizations— Renaissance paintings, Celtic coins, Pompeian paving blocks, Byzantine mosaics—all revealing, through the life of forms, a common struggle against undoing. Early in his life, at a time when Western thought was assailed by a post-World War I Spenglerian pessimism, Malraux liked to believe that civilizations saved themselves through the artistic forms they created, that humankind can overcome the terror of non-being. Increasingly, as he himself moved closer to death, he felt justified in thinking that he was right in believing that the first caveman who painted a bison or a human figure on a wall freed himself from the monsters; that every painting, every sculpture, was a victory, a lasting defiance of inevitable disappearance.

Beyond the courage of political action and virile fraternity in the cause of revolution, Malraux thus sings a more tragic courage: the courage to create, in the face of absurdity and despair, the images and the concepts that enable us to negate nothingness and to humanize the world.

Part IV · The Exit

16 · The Permanent Sabbatical

Seated on a bench with a missing slat in Paris's Parc Monceau, I muse on the sabbaticals that have punctuated my life. The park, bordered by mansions of the Belle époque, is an oasis in the opulent western sector of Paris, where long ago a village of that name existed. Its Renaissance-style arcade, its curved colonnade, its fake ruins and statues of famous people give it a touch of venerability. Claude-Nicolas Ledoux's elegant eighteenth-century tollgate rotunda is now the home of recently installed and well-frequented public toilettes. The imitation Egyptian pyramid and the Chinese fort lend the park a faint atmosphere of exoticism. The playgrounds, the manicured lawns, the shaded alleys attract mothers with their children, joggers of all ages, hugging couples on benches, as well as workers who settle there at lunchtime with their long sandwiches known as *panini*. On balmy days, groups sitting on the grass lend the scene a festive air reminiscent of Georges Seurat's painting *A Sunday on La Grande Jatte*. In the spring, when the magnolias are in bloom, the lawns are declared off limits by signs saying "au repos," at rest, meaning that one may not tread on them. From my bench I can see the narrow pond, the ducks in slow motion, the arched bridge, the children chasing one another. I watch the children in their relentless mobility, intent on their immediate desire, pleasure, or anger. They cry, they laugh, the look serious. Some of their faces already betray how they will look as adults. Some of them already look old.

Resting on my bench, I go over moments of my retirement party, nearly twenty years ago, when my colleagues at Princeton University delivered the expected speeches and I was ceremoniously handed a

gold-plated "train watch," as well as an album of testimonials. I cherish
the watch which carries on its dial, instead of the usual small hand, the
silhouette of a minuscule locomotive pulling three coaches and advanc-
ing every second, one notch at a time. When I hold it to my ear and press
a tiny button, I hear a bell and several brief whistles, followed by the
chugging of a locomotive, and then the cadenced sound of wheels on
tracks. Surrounded by noisy children at play, I hold the watch to my ear
and once again listen to the special music of the rails.

At the party, in response to my colleagues' speeches, I quipped that
my new retiree status was really the beginning of a "permanent sabbatical." I did not add that I was determined to shun self-pity, that I had pri-
vately promised to avoid replicating a scene I had so often witnessed:
namely, the sight of aging colleagues who no longer occupied offices but
continued to haunt the corridors of the department in search of welcoming faces. Some of them had been campus celebrities. Now they were
distressed because the new students and the recently appointed young
faculty did not know who they were.

The permanent sabbatical seemed a seductive idea. Real sabbaticals
came with recurrent frustrations and the apprehension that time was
running out. Was work really progressing? Like summer vacation, as every child learns, with pain, the sabbatical must come to an end. A refrain
from a novel by Virginia Woolf often rang in my ear—Mrs. Ramsay's lament in *To the Lighthouse*: "It will end, it will end." I never felt this sense
of an ending more achingly than during a sabbatical winter in Paris. Our
bedroom in the Latin Quarter gave onto a courtyard from which rose the
wailing singsong of an ambulant vendor buying and selling rags and old
clothes on certain mornings. "Habits . . . chiffons . . ." he crooned, his
morose voice scooping from low notes to almost screeching high ones.
His repeated *cri de Paris* had a chilling effect. It sounded like a lament
over relentless time, over loss even before possession.

Years ago, a mentor guided me to Montaigne, who had taught himself, in his tower-retreat, surrounded by books, to live with a sense of
loss and unraveling. Cohabitation with change, decline, and the awareness of death were themes that inspired him. Life allows for no fixity; everything is in transit. According to Montaigne, everything is in motion.
Life itself is in steady transition; it is *"movement et action."*

My admired mentor had taught me to delight in Montaigne's restless
curiosity and provocative skepticism. There was wisdom in his readiness

to accept what the flesh is heir to, as well as in his eagerness to savor life to the last drop—for, after all, as he put it, that is all we have. Montaigne observed himself in all his features and in all his moves. Yet his unremitting interest in himself never sank to self-indulgence, for he recognized that even the self and its outlook are unstable, evolving, subject to revision.

Revision (literally, seeing again) is inherent to memory. It can signify correcting, altering, transforming—and may even, in its extreme form, imply modes of denial. Rewriting our past is what most of us tend to do spontaneously. The future is unpredictable, but the past, up to a point, can be said to be unpredictable, too. Perhaps the tendency to reshape the course of events speaks of a desire to resist necessity and fate. New events alter the perception of previous ones. The archaeology of remembrance makes it difficult to decipher or interpret accurately what lies beneath the layers of the past. Even diligent digging brings up fragments at best.

Real returns to the past can be disturbing. On the sixtieth anniversary of D-day, I accompanied a Princeton delegation on a ceremonial visit to Omaha Beach in Normandy, the place where I had come ashore in June of 1944 with the Second Armored Division, nicknamed "Hell on Wheels." I can still see the half-sunk landing craft, the strewn debris, the wrecked vehicles, the abandoned ammunition belts, the anti-tank obstacles, the metal beach defenses. I can still hear the shrieking sound of the Stuka plane that strafed us during our first night on the bluff above the beach.

I had been reluctant to return to that beach and those dunes, perhaps because I thought of the many young lives lost there and remembered my own visceral fear. (The scream of the fellow hit in the head still upsets me.) But I also knew in advance that I would be irked by the touristy aspect of the on-site cemetery grounds, with their artfully planted trees, beds of roses, trimmed and well-watered lawns, ceremonial flagpoles, and neoclassical colonnades. I had read that a million visitors come each year to gaze at the disciplined rows of tombs, the Italian marble, and the bronze statue representing America's heroic young men—all this so unrelated to the realities of the invasion, the soldiers mowed down by machine-gun fire, and temporarily half-buried bodies near the dunes, wrapped in cotton mattress covers.

Much older and altogether different memories of the Normandy coast intruded themselves during my trip, carrying me back to childhood vacations in Cabourg, where I built castles in the sand and collected seashells, unaware at the time that the stately hotel right behind me was a crucial setting in a novel I discovered much later, by a writer named Marcel Proust. The return to Omaha Beach became part of a mental palimpsest onto which unrelated remembrances were scratched in time: the little boy playing in the sand, the adolescent getting a sentimental education near the mole, the helmeted soldier caught in the fury of the invasion, the Princeton administrators and trustees watching the veteran emeritus professor lay a wreath with orange flowers under the soaring war memorial. Perhaps, as one reaches the age of the permanent sabbatical, one becomes more noticeably aware that everything that lies behind us appears to be in motion and unsettled, that memories of separate periods tend to affect one another, that the past, as perceived in time, is subject to mutations.

An even more telling return to the past—a return, so to speak, full circle—seems to confirm in an uncanny way the secret workings of destiny. In 1941, a week or two after my family's safe arrival in New York Harbor on a freighter overcrowded with refugees escaping from Nazi-occupied countries, an old friend of my parents took us on an excursion to a small town in New Jersey. He parked his car on what I now know to be Witherspoon Street, near the corner facing the Princeton campus. Looking at the scene of university life before me then, I was struck by the confident gait of figures in tweed jackets moving along the alleys, carrying books and briefcases. No hurry, no somber faces. Without my realizing it at the time, a series of idyllic images settled in my mind, and I carried them with me throughout the war, all the way to devastated Berlin, where, in the fall of 1945, I determined that this was the kind of life I wanted: to live with books, to study, to learn, perchance to teach. And when, many years later, after three decades of studies and teaching in New Haven, I was beginning a second career at Princeton, I easily recognized upon arrival the site of that original scene: the corner of Witherspoon Street that I had never forgotten, as well as the sight of the historic Nassau Hall, the university's imposing administrative building, where the Continental Congress met in 1783. Here I was, after all those years, brought back by circumstances (or was it fate?) to my early vision of academic bliss.

I think so very often of Wordsworth's sonnet that extols the contentment of students in their "pensive citadels"—strongholds not for the exercise of power or for war but for the joy of studies. After almost two decades of my permanent sabbatical, the joy of teaching and learning has survived. I still feel encouraged to write and talk about the books that matter to me. But, as this last sabbatical extends in time, I also notice the telltale pockets under my eyes, the stiffness in my joints, the hearing problem, the slight dizziness and loss of balance as I walk out into the street. Nothing dramatic—at least, not so far. Just the usual afflictions of maturity. The French call it *les misères de l'âge*.

Of course, even the permanent sabbatical must come to an end. There was a time when I feared that I would not make it. Now I am distressed that I will have to give it all up. Better not to linger on the thought. According to Freud, we are really unable to believe that we are mortal, for we cannot conceive of ourselves as being absent.

The arts of dying well and ceremoniously, the *artes moriendi*, were cultivated when there was a commonly held belief in the afterlife. These so-called arts were part of a larger religious mystery. To an unbeliever, the ineluctable moment is a mystery of another kind: when and where will the grim terrorist strike?

We never speak of these matters, my wife, Bettina, and I, although we did buy a lot in a cemetery. The polished impala-black bench already carries our engraved names, together with our dates of birth. I went alone one day to visit it. The sun was out, and we were expecting friends for dinner that evening. I checked the color of the stone, but my mind moved to the wine I planned to serve at dinner. Perhaps Freud was right. Sometimes I catch myself guessing what music will be played at our memorial services. The slow movement of Mozart's clarinet concerto, or the Adagietto from Gustav Mahler's Fifth Symphony? What will our children decide? In my mind, I see myself actually present at my own service. My absence is inconceivable.

As a child, in late summer, I used to listen to the buzzing of the large end-of-season flies dashing from one side of my room to the other, bumping against a window or a wall. Someone called it the summer chamber music. Ever since my childhood, the memory of these boisterous flies has had a special meaning. Their buzzing and frantic to-and-fro bustle announce the end of the summer. The end of the vacation. *It will end, it will end.*

A passage at the beginning of Thomas Mann's *Death in Venice* keeps echoing in my mind. It depicts Aschenbach's crossing of the silent lagoon as he is being rowed in a black gondola toward the Lido. Even as he conjures up ominous images of being ferried to the Kingdom of Hades, he feels overcome by a spell of indolence, and surrenders to the wish that the voyage might last forever. This page continues to resonate with me, for I remember that as a child, in love with trains, sitting gently rocked and half-asleep next to my parents in a train compartment, listening to the poetic cadences of wheels on rails, I knew because of the slowing down of the soothing rhythm that we were approaching the home station, and I did not want to arrive.

Acknowledgments

Many friends, students, and colleagues have stimulated and encouraged me. Warm thanks go to Esther Roush, who has assisted me in various ways, with dedication and utmost competence, in the preparation of this collection of essays.

Special thanks are due to Alan Thomas, Editorial Director at the University of Chicago Press, who has guided me over the years with wisdom and encouragement. My gratitude also goes to Randolph Petilos, who was most helpful, as he has been in the past, during the entire preparation of the manuscript. And as always, my agent Chris Calhoun set high standards with his literary taste and thorough professionalism.

My greatest debt is to my wife Beth, who has been my attentive and demanding reader. Her judicious comments and sharp critical sense have been a steady challenge.

· · ·

The following chapters have appeared as independent essays, in some cases in a somewhat different, longer, or shorter form, in the following publications: A number of sections of chapter 1, "The Pensive Citadel," were originally published in *The Yale Review* (January 2014). Chapter 2, "Between Two Worlds," originally appeared in *The Hudson Review* 68, no. 3 (Autumn 2015); chapter 3, "What Existentialism Meant to Us," in *Yale French Studies* nos. 135 and 136 (2019); chapter 4, "Cleopatra at Yale" (in quite a different form), in *Raritan* (Winter 2019); chapter 5, "Brombingo!—Learning from Students," in *Raritan* (Summer 2021);

chapter 7, "In Praise of Jealousy?" in *Raritan* (Fall 2020); chapter 8, "On Rereading," in *The Yale Review* (Spring 2021); chapter 9, "Lessons of Montaigne," in *The Hudson Review* 75, no. 1 (Spring 2022); chapter 10, "The Audacities of Molière's Don Juan," in *The Hudson Review* 74, no. 2 (Summer 2021); chapter 12, "Encounters with Monsieur Beyle," in *Stendhal* by Victor Brombert (Chicago: University of Chicago Press, 2017). Some elements of chapter 15, "Malraux and the World of Violence," were originally presented at a symposium in honor of André Malraux, April 15–16, 1977, at Skidmore College, and published in *Dialogues with the Unseen and the Unknown: Essays in Memory of André Malraux*, ed. Lynne L. Gelber, (Saratoga Springs, NY: The Skidmore College Department of Modern Languages and Literature, 1978). Chapter 16, "The Permanent Sabbatical," originally appeared online in *The New Yorker* (January 16, 2018).

Index

Achilles, 126
Action Française movement, 21
Adorno, Theodor, ix–x
Aeschylus, 53; *Agamemnon*, 38; *Oresteia, The*, 34
Andromache, 126
anti-Semitism, 22–23, 27, 29, 55, 133–34
Ariosto, Ludovico, 114–15
Aristotle, 20, 91, 99
Augustus, 49
Auschwitz, 33

Balzac, Honoré de, 83, 121, 130
Barthes, Roland, 9
Bastille: assault on, 133; fall of, 128, 132; myth of, 132
Battle of the Bulge, 6, 14, 16
Baty, Gaston, 30
Baudelaire, 8, 24, 26, 28, 36; anonymity, in the crowd, 120; "Any Where Out of the World," 125; "Au lecteur," 123; "À une heure du matin" (At 1:00 a.m.), 120; beauty, ephemeral nature of, 124; bizarre and ugly, attraction to, 124; "Brumes et pluies" (Fog and Rain), 122; "Crépuscule du soir" (Dusk), 122; "Éloge du maquillage" (In Praise of Makeup), 44, 125; evil, as natural, 125; as flâneur, xi–xii, 31, 81, 118, 120–21, 126; "Heroism of Modern Life, The,"

121; incognito, cultivating art of, 120; *La Fanfarlo*, 122, 125; "Le cygne" (The Swan), 118, 126; "Le mauvais vitrier" (The Bad Glazier), 119; *Les fleurs du mal* (The Flowers of Evil), 118, 122; "Les foules" (The Crowds), 120, 126; "Le soleil," 122; "Les phares," 122; "Le spleen de Paris," 122–23; "Les sept vieillards" (The Seven Old Men), 121; "L'irrémédiable," 124; lodging, distaste for, 120; makeup, praise of, 125; modernity of, 126; modernity, and sense of beauty, 121; Mother Nature, distaste for, 124–25; *Painter of Modern Life, The*, 123; Paris of, 118–24, 126; pleasure in movement, 124; "Rêve parisien" (Parisian Dream), 125–26; "Salon de 1846," 124; surrealism of, 125–26; *Tableaux parisiens*, 121; as tireless stroller, 120; urban crowds and cityscapes, 126–27
Beaumarchais, Pierre-Augustin Caron de, 62
Beauvoir, Simone de, 34, 36; *Le sang des autres* (*The Blood of Others*), 32
Beckett, Samuel, 102
Beethoven, Ludwig van: Eroica symphony (Symphony no. 3), 16
Bellini, Vincenzo: *Norma*, 16
Benjamin, Walter, 129